WINTER BACKPACKING

Your Guide to Safe and Warm Winter Camping and Day Trips

BEN SHILLINGTON

Photos by: Trevor Lush

THE HELICONIA PRESS

Distributed by
Gordon Soules Book Publishers Ltd.
1359 Ambleside Lane,
West Vancouver, BC, Canada V7T 2Y9
books@gordonsoules.com
604-922-6588 Fax: 604-688-5442

Published by

The Heliconia Press, Inc.

1576 Beachburg Road, Beachburg, Ontario K0J 1C0 Canada

www.helipress.com

Written by: Ben Shillington

Project Managed by: Amy Luscombe

Edited by: Tim Shuff and Rebecca Sandiford

Photography by: Trevor Lush except as noted.

Design and Layout by: Betty Biesenthal (Design House)

Library and Archives Canada Cataloguing in Publication.

Shillington, Ben 1982-

     Winter Backpacking: Your Guide to Safe and Warm Winter Camping and Day Trips Ben Shillington.

ISBN 978-1-896980-41-6

     1. Snow camping. 2. Snow camping--Equipment and supplies.

I. Title.

GV198.9.S55 2009   796.54   C2008-907170-0

About Safety

Winter camping is an activity with inherent risks, and this book is designed as a general guide, not a substitute for experience. The publisher and the author do not take responsibility for the use of any of the materials or methods described in this book. By following any of the procedures described within, you do so at your own risk.

18.56

Dec 16/09

TABLE OF CONTENTS

Introduction

A Christmas Story

Foreword

Acknowledgments

Keeping Warm

How You Lose Heat 1

Clothing 2

Sleeping Systems 13

Decisions, Decisions 22

Cooking & Eating

Winter Nutrition 25

Creating a Trip Menu 34

Packing Your Food 42

Stoves 43

Backpacks, Packing & Equipment

Backpacks: A New Piece of Anatomy 49

How to Pack a Backpack 56

Packing Options and Technique 62

Sleds or Pulks: An Alternative to Backpacks 64

Winter Travel

Hiking in Your Boots 67

Snowshoeing *69*

Cross-Country Skiing *77*

Getting Around in the Mountains *80*

Skijoring. *86*

Dog Sledding *87*

Winter Camp

The Camp Triangle *89*

Shelters *90*

Setting Up Your Bed *100*

The Camp Kitchen. *101*

Building a Fire *103*

The Camp Bathroom. *107*

Bedtime Routine *108*

Navigation

The Compass *112*

Topographic Maps. *113*

Magnetic North and Declination *113*

Using a Map and Compass *114*

Winter Hazards & First Aid

Dehydration. *122*

Hypothermia *122*

Frostbite. *125*

Sunburn and Snow Blindness. *126*

Immersion Foot 127

Blisters 127

Your Winter First Aid Kit 128

Winter Survival

Leave a Trip Plan 132

Nine Steps to Survival 132

Emergency Shelters 136

Survival Kit 137

Good Company: Kids & Dogs

Winter Backpacking with Children 139

Winter Backpacking with Dogs 143

Plan Your Trip and Do It!

Get Out There and Camp! 151

Appendix: Packing Lists

Day Hike Gear 155

Sleeping Gear 156

Active Clothing 156

Dry Clothing 157

Cooking Equipment 157

Shelter Equipment 158

Winter-Specific Equipment 158

Miscellaneous Gear 159

Personal and Hygiene: 159

ABOUT THE AUTHOR

Ben Shillington is an experienced outdoor recreation instructor and guide who has led multiple mountaineering, mountain biking, whitewater and flat water canoe expeditions. In 2003, Ben was invited to be a mountain climber for the Discovery Channel's Mount Everest Expedition, where he spent two months climbing and filming the western crown of Mount Everest up to Base Camp II (21,325 feet; 6,500 meters). Ben has summited a 21,000-foot (6,400-meter) peak in the Himalayas, trekked independently to Everest's Base Camp, and guided on Mount Kilimanjaro.

INTRODUCTION

If you've picked up this book, you're either new to winter backpacking, interested in giving winter camping a try, or a seasoned winter backpacker looking to make your adventures into the wilderness more comfortable.

Well, having been a winter backpacking and camping enthusiast and instructor for years, I couldn't feel more confident in assuring you that with a little preparation, it's amazing how warm, fun and comfortable it can be. Far more interesting than spending time in a gym, winter backpacking is also a great way to get exercise and improve your fitness level during the cold months. It's also a terrific way to get outside with friends and family and make the most out of the shorter winter days. On top of these great reasons to give winter backpacking a try, you should know that there is a lot of excitement and satisfaction to be had in knowing that you have the ability and the skills to survive—and enjoy—a full day outing or overnight campout in the winter.

Many people think that to go backpacking or camping in the winter you need to be "hard core"—that you need lots of fancy, expensive gear, and that you should be ready to suffer. None of this is true. Whether you are planning your first winter overnighter, or fine-tuning skills you have already developed from previous adventures, there are simply a few key components that will help to make your winter backpacking trip a success. You need to have a positive mindset, set realistic goals, and properly plan for your trip.

Getting in a positive mindset starts the minute you come up with the idea of heading into the wilderness in sub-zero temperatures. Get excited about your upcoming adventure!

Setting realistic goals takes into account a variety of elements, including your fitness level and the environment you'll be entering.

Proper planning for a trip is the key component to success and it involves educating yourself so that you can make important decisions. Before leaving on your trip, ask yourself about such things like: When, where and for how long do I want to go? Who will I go with? Will I take the dog or the kids? How will I get there? How much food do I need and how will I get drinking water? Do I have the proper equipment? How will I stay warm? What type of terrain will I be camping in?

I wrote this book to help you with all these things and to make your winter backpacking experience as fun, safe and comfortable as possible. It should be noted that although this book offers a comprehensive look at most issues relating to winter backpacking, it was necessary to cut short the topic of mountain travel in avalanche prone areas, as this topic requires a much greater knowledge base, including such things as the use of specialized equipment and the ability to read weather and snow conditions. There are some great publications already available on this topic, although I would highly recommend going a step further and taking a course on backcountry mountain travel if this is something you wish to pursue.

Although I'm very proud of this book, all books have their limitations and can only take you so far. Practical experience is the key to ensuring your winter backpacking trips roll as smoothly as possible, so the obvious next step is to just go and do it! And with that said, welcome to the exciting world of winter backpacking!

A Christmas Story

Somewhere around age 12 or 13, I decided that I was going to be an outdoor adventure guide and lead expeditions for a living. My transportation would be self-propelled, which would get me super fit. I was going to be hard core and learn everything that I could about wilderness travel so that I could journey all over the world.

I also swore to never again wear a pair of jeans because I learned that they are impractical for camping. (It's been 14 years now!) Anyway, from that point on, my focus was on getting any wilderness experience that I could. My major passion was for mountain biking but I also had a big attraction to mountaineering and figured that someday I would do that too. Then I realized that if I was going to do all this stuff, I needed to start training immediately!

Back around that time, I remember seeing a book at the Barry's Bay drug store called *The Climb* by Anatoli Boukreev about a mountaineering trip on Mount Everest. I looked at this book every time I was in town with my mother. I would check out all the pictures and imagine myself in the mountains, sleeping in the snow, battling out huge blizzards, and climbing for days and weeks on end. I also decided that the training for my inevitable adventures was going to start that Christmas Eve with a winter campout.

I don't think my parents were too keen on me sleeping outside in -20°F (-30°C) weather, especially without any real gear to speak of, but I suppose they thought that as soon as I got cold, I would just head back into the house and curl up beside the fireplace or climb into my bed.

Well, that first campout on Christmas Eve is definitely one I will never forget, and not only because I learned a lot about the mechanisms of heat loss! (An important thing to know about that is covered in Chapter 1 of this book.) I told my parents that since a full night's sleep was considered to be eight hours, that that was how long I intended to be outside before coming in for breakfast. I dug out a bit of a coffin shelter, about 3 feet wide, 1/2-foot deep and about 6 feet long, which was just a little bit bigger than my body. I had no sleeping bag, no sleeping pad, no tent, no tarp, no shelter. I was setting my self up for a loooooong eight hours.

What I did have was a rectangular piece of plastic, the kind that is used as a vapor barrier liner for walls in home construction. This plastic with a folded blanket on top served as my ground pad. I had an itchy horse blanket and an old synthetic comforter that I folded together and wrapped around my body in lieu of a sleeping bag. I wore a wool hat but I can't remember what I wore on my body to sleep in.

It was cold, but what a beautiful night lying out there under a clear and starry sky! I kept myself motivated by imagining the trips and adventures I might go on some day, climbing big mountains in far-off places. It probably also helped that I kept pumping up my ego by telling myself how hard core I was. I mean, if people around town thought that the Madawaska Valley Hockey League was hard core, what about being a mountaineer? I froze my ass off that night and didn't sleep much at all, but I stuck it out the whole eight hours. At that point in my life, it was one of the most exciting and rewarding things I'd ever done. I felt sure that having made it through the whole night in really cold conditions with minimal gear, I could be a mountaineer. I mean, if I could survive that, I could survive anything!

Heading into the house that Christmas morning, I felt like a true adventurer, bursting with pride, and left my plastic and blankets out in the snow in the front yard as a trophy for my grandparents and uncles to see when they arrived. I wouldn't admit how cold I had been and still was, but I think the way I gulped down a hot cup of coffee as soon as I got inside might have given me away a little.

I have made it a tradition to sleep out every Christmas Eve since then. Over the years, I have learned so much more about outdoor recreation and how easy it is to stay warm in cold weather with proper gear and preparation, but winter camping is still one of my favorite things to do, and I hope you discover that you love it too!

FOREWORD

The wind tore into the side of the tent. It was insistent and violent. It had started somewhere as a little breeze on the Tibetan Plateau, but on its journey to our camp at over 21,000 feet on the side of Mount Everest, it had matured and gained strength. It was a hard wind in a very hard place, cold and unforgiving.

Ben Shillington, the author of this book, was at the camp with me that night, sharing in the sometimes questionable joy of mountaineering. We lay in our tents, holding our emotions in a delicate balance between fear and confidence. The dread that we felt from knowing that a much more powerful force than ourselves was at play was mixed with the calm of knowing that we had the skills to manage it and make good decisions. This is the golden reward of experience: nuggets of information get stored away over time, building a wealth of knowledge that you can draw upon when you need to.

For the uninitiated, winter camping can be intimidating. It takes two hard things, winter and camping, and puts them together to make something that seems even harder. The idea of purposefully placing yourself with limited equipment in harsh conditions might seem daunting at first, but it doesn't have to be hard or scary at all—in fact, you can have a really good time—if you take the time to learn how to do it properly!

I have known Ben Shillington for many years. He's an expert not only on how to stay alive in winter conditions but on how to thrive in them as well. As you pick up this book, you can have faith that its contents will give you the information you need to have a safe, comfortable and fun winter backpacking experience. Remember, the season that appears solemn in its silence is not dead but only sleeping, yours to awaken and enjoy! The commandments of winter are before you. Let Shillington part the seas of anxiety and confusion and lead you to the winter promised land. Once you're there, rejoice and shout praise. In Ben we trust!

ABOUT BEN WEBSTER

Ben Webster is one of the world's most accomplished expedition leaders. In a career spanning over 25 years of high adventure, he has led over 30 major expeditions on six continents, summiting famous peaks, leading first ascents of climbs and first descents of whitewater rivers. He is also an acclaimed television producer, documentary filmmaker and photojournalist. Among his notable undertakings, Ben has led five successful and major multimedia expeditions on Mount Everest where he has not only reached the summit but also produced the first live television broadcast from the mountain back to North American networks including ABC and CTV. From the barren tundra in the Artic to the steamy jungles of Borneo and all points in between, Ben has literally 'been there and done that.' He's also a really nice guy.

ACKNOWLEDGMENTS

I would like to dedicate this book to my mother and father, Harold and Dawn Shillington, who have sacrificed many things in their lives for me. I want to thank you for moving our family to the Ottawa Valley so that I wouldn't have to grow up in a city. Thank you for always standing beside me 100%, always encouraging me to follow my dreams no matter how crazy, and for always supporting me in my less than common career in the outdoor adventure industry. You are always on my mind.

A big thank you to my girlfriend Robyn Phillips for always supporting my crazy adventures, and my sometimes long and very frequent absences out in the field; for letting me be me. You are my biggest motivator and you provide me with the drive that I need to accomplish many of the goals I set.

I also wanted to take a moment to send a huge thanks to the companies who provided gear to use during the production of this book. Know that your gear has found a loving home and is being enjoyed immensely! In particular, thanks to Mountain Hardwear for fulfilling our dreams and providing all the great clothing, backpacking and camping gear. We couldn't have been more comfortable during our long days and nights outside! A big thanks also goes to MSR for supplying their superb snowshoes and stoves, and to Thermarest for supplying the sleeping pads. Special thanks also goes to MEC, as the kids are still beaming with their new winter clothing, and if our dogs could speak, I know they would be communicating their immense appreciation to Pet Edge for their winter clothing and sleeping gear. A final and sincere thanks goes to Harvest Foodworks for supplying the hearty camping meals that kept our energy and spirits high during long days of shooting.

KEEPING WARM

Of course, keeping warm day or night is one of the highest priorities for anyone heading out on a winter backpacking adventure. Let's look at how it's done.

How You Lose Heat

If you understand how your body loses heat, you can be prepared to manage heat loss and stay at a comfortable temperature.

• *Conduction* heat loss is caused by direct contact with something else that is colder than you. For example, you'll lose heat through conduction by lying on snow without an insulating barrier like a foam pad, or by holding onto a metal fuel bottle with bare hands.

• *Convection* heat loss is caused by air or water moving around your body. Think of how a warm day feels cooler when a breeze blows. Convection heat loss will also be at work if you have cold, damp clothing next to your skin. Convection heat loss is minimized by wearing proper clothing and having suitable shelter.

• *Radiation* heat loss is the loss of heat through the infrared wavelengths given off by any object; the warmer the object, the more it gives off. Heat rises off your body the same way that heat radiates from a wood stove. Radiation heat loss is also minimized with proper clothing and shelter.

• *Evaporation* heat loss is caused by perspiring—your sweat evaporates as hot vapor in cold dry air, taking your body heat with it.

Chapter 1

How You Lose Heat

Clothing

Sleeping Systems

Decisions, Decisions

Balaclavas not only make you look sinister but they provide insulation and help warm up the air that you inhale.

Donning a down jacket just as you are cooling down after the day's activity will keep you cozy until bed time.

• **Respiration** heat loss is simply the loss of heat through breathing. With every exhalation your body loses the warmth of the air from your lungs, and with every inhalation takes in colder air that needs to be warmed. Of course, you can't stop breathing, but if you are feeling cold, you can try covering your mouth and nose with a breathable layer like a scarf, balaclava or neck warmer.

• **Urination** (or lack thereof) – If you let your bladder stay full, your body has to work harder to keep the urine warm. This robs heat from your body starting with your extremities (hands and feet), making them more susceptible to frost nip or frostbite. Relieve yourself regularly and you'll stay warmer.

While it's important to be aware of all of the above, being exposed to wind and wetness are the two fastest ways you'll lose heat doing any outdoors activity because convection in these forms draws heat away from your body faster than it can be produced. The good news is that with a little preparation (meaning, proper clothing, and enough of it), you can minimize convection heat loss and stay warm.

Clothing

To minimize heat loss, you need to be able to both conserve and regulate your body heat, as well keep yourself dry. Much of this is accomplished by layering your clothing. To minimize the build-up of moisture in your clothing, put layers on as your body cools and take layers off as your body warms up—ideally before you start to sweat.

Clothing Layers

Your layering system should consist of three or more layers: the base layer, the insulating layer and the shell layer. These will often be made of different materials to suit their different purposes. Instead of paying a few hundred dollars for one heavy ski or snowmobile jacket, you can spend about the same amount in total and get one garment in each of the three layering categories. The beauty of using a layering system is that you can make different combinations to accommodate any outdoor activity, no matter what the season or temperature. Over time, adding to your layering system wardrobe will give you even more combinations and options.

Let's start with a discussion of the basic three-layer system, and the variety of materials that can be used for each layer.

Base Layer

The base layer is also known as the wicking layer and is worn in direct contact with your bare skin. This means your underwear, as well as long underwear, top and bottom. (Women and cross-dressing men should also consider their bra as part of this layer.) The base layer should fit snugly—almost like a second skin—but not restrict your movement in any way.

The main function of the base layer is to keep your skin dry and move moisture (from perspiration or otherwise) away from your body. The fabric used should absorb water but not retain it, which typically means a synthetic material like polyester or polypropylene. High-quality merino wool has become popular lately as an alternative to these synthetic fibers. Although wool offers a slightly higher warmth-to-weight ratio than polypropylene and has natural odor-resistant properties—an advantage when you're winter camping for many nights without a shower—it absorbs more moisture and takes longer to dry. Synthetics are typically the better choice for sweaty, high-energy activities.

When choosing a base layer, you'll find that most manufacturers offer options of lightweight, mid-weight and heavy-weight base layers. Weight refers to the thickness of a garment. Lightweight is best suited for high aerobic activity; mid-weight is good for repetitive stop-and-go activity, and heavy-weight is best suited for very cold temperatures and moderate to low levels of activity.

Never use cotton as a base layer. There is an old saying that you'd be well-advised to remember: "cotton kills." While cotton is great for absorbing moisture, it also retains moisture extremely well and, once damp, loses its insulating properties and becomes a

A heavy-weight base layer is ideal for low levels of activity, like snoozing.

Female friends have advised me about the best winter activity bras. While fleece bras are cozy for wearing around camp, the best winter bras for physical activity will have two layers built in: a wicking layer to keep moisture away from your skin, and an insulating layer that might also offer a little extra wind protection. This combination of breathability, wicking and insulation will keep you warm and comfortable when you're on the move.

Whatever middle or outer layer you choose, consider garments with full leg or armpit zippers, which will allow you to ventilate easily.

Soft shells create a windproof, exceptionally weather-resistant outer layer great for high energy activities.

cold-conductor. Wearing damp cotton, you'll lose body heat rapidly, which can lead to hypothermia.

Middle Layer

The middle layer should provide reliable insulation by trapping warm air and keeping this warmth close to your body. This insulating layer must efficiently retain your body heat, but also "breathe," allowing the moisture given off by your body to escape so that you can stay dry. Middle-layer garments should fit closely but not restrict movement.

As with your base layer, you have options of light-, mid- and heavy-weight insulating layers, and the same selection principles apply. Again, synthetic materials, such as fleece or pile, are a good choice for this layer. You can also wear wool or down-filled clothing for this layer.

Outer Layer

The outer layer should protect you from the elements, reducing your exposure to rain, snow and wind. This layer is responsible for minimizing heat loss from conduction, convection, radiation and evaporation. Your protective outer shell can range from a simple nylon windbreaker or rubber rain suit to a more expensive three-ply waterproof breathable garment like Gore-Tex. Waterproof breathable shells can keep you drier by letting the moisture vapor out, while not letting water from rain or snow in.

You don't just want a shell jacket, but also pants. Bib pants with suspenders are especially good; they keep the snow out when you fall in thigh-deep powder trying to perfect those backcountry turns.

Soft Shells

An exception to the traditional three-layer system is the soft shell jacket. "Soft shells" are made of a soft, stretchy material that combines the insulation and breathability of a middle layer with the wind- and water-resistance of an outer layer. Soft shells are popular because they are very versatile for all kinds of situations where you don't need a completely waterproof jacket—especially aerobic activities where you may be too hot to wear a shell but it's too windy or snowy to wear only a fleece. Although a soft shell can replace your middle and outer layers in such situations, it still helps to think in terms of a three-layer system: What will transport moisture away from my body? What will provide my insulation? What will protect me from wind, rain and snow? Even if you opt for a soft shell, it's always a good idea to carry a traditional, waterproof shell in case of really nasty weather.

Clothing Materials

The following chart shows the basic advantages and disadvantages of popular clothing materials for the three main layers.

BASE LAYERS - Wicking Materials

MATERIAL	ADVANTAGES	DISADVANTAGES
Polyester	• water repellent • dries quickly • abrasion resistant • non-allergenic	• can get smelly (retains body odor)
Polypropylene	• water repellent • dries quickly • abrasion resistant • non-allergenic • warm when wet	• can get really smelly (retains body odor)
Merino Wool	• very comfortable against the skin • warm when wet • odor-resistant • natural fiber	• heavy when wet • longer drying time • more expensive
	Fans of merino wool claim that it keeps you warm when you're cold and cools you down when you're too warm – a great temperature regulator.	
Silk	• very comfortable against the skin • very light to pack • natural fiber • wicks moisture adequately	• not very durable • can require special care • not as warm as wool or synthetics
	Silk long underwear can make a great set of camping pajamas!	
Spandex	• non-allergenic • form-fitting	• tight fit • hot

MIDDLE LAYERS - Insulating Materials

MATERIAL	ADVANTAGES	DISADVANTAGES
Fleece	• affordable • warm • insulates when wet • dries quickly • non-allergenic	• bulkier to pack than down or Poly-fil • heavy when wet
	Fleece comes in weights rated 100, 200 and 300 from light to heavy. It is also available in windproof varieties.	
Wool	• warm when wet • odor-resistant • natural fiber	• heavy when wet • long drying time
Down	• excellent warmth-to-weight ratio • lasts a lifetime • natural fiber	• expensive initial cost • zero insulation value when wet • takes forever to dry • takes more time to clean • some people are allergic to down
	If you can afford it and are willing to be vigilant about keeping down dry, it is one of the best insulators around.	

Synthetic fills (i.e. Poly-fil)	• non-allergenic • lighter and more compact than fleece	• will lose loft and insulating value over time; short lifespan
Cotton	• very absorbent • keeps you cool • natural fiber *Cotton is NEVER suitable for winter camping!*	• very cold when wet • takes forever to dry

OUTER LAYERS - Shell Materials

MATERIAL	ADVANTAGES	DISADVANTAGES
Nylon	• very durable • light • compact • affordable • non-allergenic • can be made windproof or water-resistant with coatings and laminates.	• highly flammable
Gore-Tex	• waterproof and breathable • lightweight • multiple uses • durable *Gore-Tex comes in 2-ply and 3-ply options, with 3-ply being more durable and breathable (at greater cost), and 2-ply being more affordable and less durable..*	• can be expensive • needs lots of maintenance
Soft Shells	• combine all three layers in one • more wind- and water-resistant than a mid-layer; more breathable than a shell • comfortable for a wide range of temperatures and activities *Many different brand names, materials and styles to choose from, each with different performance properties.*	• not fully waterproof • better on short or day trips • better in more stable weather

Putting Together Your Winter Clothing System

When you're putting together your winter layering system and deciding what clothes to bring, it helps to divide clothes into two categories: active clothes and dry clothes.

Active Clothes

Active clothes consist of everything that you need to wear to stay warm while on the move: base, insulating and shell layers. The objective is to stay warm but also dry from perspiration and precipitation.

Dry Clothes

Dry clothes are the clothes that will always be packed and waterproofed until the end of the day when you are in camp. These select few pieces of clothing will be packed away pretty much anytime you plan to venture much farther than 10 feet from your tent. Your dry clothes are your safe haven and peace of mind. An extra pair of heavy long johns and a heavy synthetic long-sleeve shirt are usually all you need for dry clothes.

Extra Clothes

One thing that many people don't realize is that you should have roughly the same amount of clothing whether you are heading out for two days or seven. You will basically wear the same set of active clothing layers every day, so you don't need any extra T-shirts or even a pair of pants (since on your legs, your first layer is your long johns, then your fleece insulation, then your shell pants). Your dry clothes are never going to get wet from perspiration or precipitation, so why pack any extra?

There are, however, a few exceptions to the rule of minimizing extra clothes. You will want to pack extra pairs of dry socks so that you can rotate them while damp pairs are drying. You should also make sure that you pack one extra pair of mitts or gloves and an extra warm hat so that if you lose or soak one of these critical pieces of equipment, you won't be exposing your ears and fingers to frostbite.

Down Jacket

I haven't mentioned down jackets yet because they are sort of in a class of their own, doing double duty as a daytime layer and an evening layer.

This may be one of the most important pieces of safety equipment you'll bring. Don't wear it during the day (unless daytime temperatures are much colder than you anticipated),

No matter how hard, wet or cold the day is, with dry clothes packed away you will always know that you have a nice cozy outfit to sport in your tent.

Good quality mitts and gloves often have 'dummy strings' attached to help avoid situations like this, but they only work when used.

but rather use it to stay warm at camp or during lunch breaks when your body temperature can drop quickly after physical activity and exertion. Keep your down jacket accessible, but in a waterproof stuff sack to make sure it stays dry for when you really need it.

I'll talk a little more about down in the section ahead on *Sleeping Systems*.

Finding Clothes: Shopping, Scavenging and Sewing

There are lots of ways to put together your three layers, including buying new clothing, finding clothing that you already have that is suitable, and finally, if you're handy at sewing, altering articles you already have to make them more suitable.

Shopping for New Things

Your first time heading into an outdoor gear and clothing store can be overwhelming, but it doesn't have to be if you know what you are looking for. Here are a few things to consider.

Cotton is cotton, fleece is fleece and Gore-Tex is Gore-Tex, so why is there such a huge price gap between so many garments that seem to be almost identical? Like anything, there are different degrees of quality, but remember that you can end up paying a lot for a brand name. You will also pay more for bells and whistles like extra Velcro tabs and zippers, pockets, toggles, custom work, varieties of color, and other little features. Anytime a manufacturer adds a feature, the price goes up for the increased labor involved.

You have to decide which of these features will provide real value to you. For example, you might be faced with a choice between a basic pair of mid-weight fleece pants for one price, or the same pants with full-length leg zippers for 30% more. They're the same material and fit, but the zippers will let you ventilate when you get too hot, rather than struggling to take your pants off. Alternately, when looking at jackets, you might have the option of paying significantly more for one with a lot of zippered pockets. Zippers and seam-sealing on pockets add a lot of bulk and expense to a jacket, and you may just end up being confused about which pocket to search for your energy bar or lip balm. But then again, you may be a very organized person who likes to carry a lot of items in different places on your body. Think about what you really need, and develop a system and philosophy that works for you.

What's in Your Closet?

Before you head out and buy a whole bunch of new clothing, take a look at what you already have in your closet. Using the information in this chapter about the different fabrics that are effective in a layering system, look at the clothing tags and see what you can use.

You might already have a windbreaker and maybe a fleece sweater or jacket. One or two of your long-sleeved shirts might be made out of 100% polyester, or a poly-acrylic

If you're on a budget, check out second-hand and thrift stores. It's amazing how much nylon, fleece and polyester clothing you can find at these stores—perfectly good stuff for a fraction of the cost!

blend. The same applies for pants and long johns. Check to see if you have a pair of pants made of nylon or some other type of 100% synthetic material, or a light pair of rain pants. Just remember: no cotton, not even cotton blends.

Alterations to Clothes You Already Own

The clothing that you already have (or just bought at a second-hand store) might not be very fancy, but as long as it's going to do the job and get you out in the winter, who cares?

If you are good with a sewing machine or even needle and thread, consider the following possible alterations:

- Turn a fleece pullover into a full-front zip
- Put some Velcro tabs on the cuffs of your fleece jackets or pant legs
- Add an elastic pull cord around the bottom of a sweater or jacket to help keep out drafts
- Cut and sew in armpit zippers on a fleece or full-length leg zippers on a pair of pants for ventilation

Hands and Feet: Taking Care of Your Extremities

As soon as your hands or feet are cold, it's hard to think about or enjoy anything else. Some people also seem to have a tendency to get cold feet and hands more easily than others. Fortunately, with a little preparation it's easy to keep your digits warm!

When you remove your mitts or gloves for more than a moment, slip them inside your jacket to rest on your shoulders. This will keep them warmer from your body heat than if you stuffed them in your pockets. If they are slightly damp, you will find that they often dry off fairly quickly in this unusual spot. If you make it a habit, you will always know where your mitts or gloves are.

The key to keeping your feet warm is blood circulation. Don't try to add warmth by wearing a super-thick sock or adding extra pairs. Keep your boots fairly loose and wear one pair of mid-weight synthetic or wool (not cotton) socks.

Mitts and Gloves: Keeping Your Hands Warm

Using two or three layers is also useful when it comes to keeping your hands warm. Material choices for the different layers of hand protection are typically the same as they are for other clothing layers. Everybody seems to find a combination that works for them. If you don't know what works for you, try out some systems on some day trips before you go winter camping. Some popular combinations include: thin wicking liner with an insulating, protective shell; thin wicking layer, a thicker insulating layer, and a shell layer on top; and a fleece or wool layer next-to-skin with a shell on top.

Mitts are warmer than gloves because your fingers can share heat with each other in the common space they share. The drawback, of course, is that you can't use your fingers as easily. Some people get around this by wearing a glove liner or fleece glove with an over-mitt for the shell. That way, you can take off the over-mitt easily and use your gloved hands to do things that require manual dexterity, while the over-mitt shell helps to keep the warmth of your fingers together.

Footwear: Don't Get Cold Feet

In the winter, as long as you are moving and have some way to keep the snow from entering your footwear, you can often keep your feet warm in almost anything. The real challenge is keeping your feet warm when you're at rest.

You can't go wrong with a good, sturdy pair of snow boots. Classic high-top winter boots will work really well in most conditions, as long as they fit your feet properly, are comfortable and well-insulated. (Popular brands are Baffin and Sorel.) High-top winter boots have a waterproof rubber sole and toe box, and a very high nylon or leather calf with an enclosure that will help to keep snow from entering your boots and melting. These boots also usually have removable, insulated felt liners. Sometimes you can even upgrade the liners to a warmer pair, and when they get worn out you only need to re-place the liners instead of the whole boot.

Now, you don't necessarily have to go out and get a brand new pair of snow boots to head out on a winter hike or campout. You may already have a pair of everyday footwear that will work just fine as a four-season boot with a little modification. A sturdy, mid-weight leather hiking boot with a full gusseted tongue works well for winter hiking and snowshoeing. They provide good ankle support and the gusseted tongue keeps water and snow out of your boots. The only downfall to leather hikers is that most of them are not insulated, so extra care must be taken to ensure the warmth of your feet. If you have a pair of leather hiking boots that are already broken in, here is a recipe for converting them into a winter boot:

1. Waterproof the leather with a boot wax from your local outdoor store. Do two or three treatments and let it cure properly.

There are a variety of fairly inexpensive hand warmers that you can bring along just in case your hands get really cold and you need to warm them up fast, such as to prevent frostnip or frostbite. Some warmers are disposable and some are reusable. I recommend the reusable ones to cut down on environmental waste. Most types last anywhere from about half an hour to a couple of hours. In non-emergency situations, they are good for a blast of comfort if your hands get unexpectedly cold. I have also known friends who have thrown these down their shirts or bras, and placed them against chilly feet once bundled in their sleeping bags.

2. Slip on a single pair of your favorite pair of mid-weight merino wool or synthetic socks (yes, just one pair).

3. Lace up the boots according to the outside temperature: lightly if weather is very cold; more snugly if weather is only mildly cold.

4. Add a pair of high-cut gaiters in your choice of style and color.

5. Grab a cup of your favorite hot drink (my preference would be a tasty dark roast, brewed strong) and get out in the snow.

What's a Gaiter?

A gaiter is a tube of durable material that fits snugly around the top of your boot and extends up your leg to keep water, snow, mud and debris from entering the top of your footwear. Most gaiters close around the leg with either a full-length zipper or Velcro, have a cord or elastic around the top, and a rubber strap that passes under the boot sole to attach them to the boot. There are many different styles and designs. Heights vary from ankle-high to knee-high, and materials can be anything from plain nylon to Gore-Tex, or even specialty materials like ballistic nylon that is designed to resist being shredded by mountaineering and ice climbing crampons. Prices range from as little as $15 for a plain nylon gaiter to $150 for something fancy. Do a little research and ask

Left: Leather hikers are great for winter camping when coupled with high-cut gaiters that help keep snow out and warmth in. Right: Removable liners are a terrific feature of any winter boot because if they get wet from snow or sweat, you can simply remove them in the evening and dry them out near the fire or in the foot of your sleeping bag.

Boots often get wet even when they are thoroughly waterproofed. That's because feet sweat. If you want to keep your boots from getting wet from the inside out, make yourself a homemade pair of vapor-barrier liner socks! VBL socks trap moisture from your feet before it can soak into your boot liners. You can spend up to 100 dollars for a fancy pair of VBL socks or make a pair by pulling two grocery or bread bags overtop of each socked foot before putting on your boots. Be sure to pack a few extra grocery bags for the trip!

the staff at your outdoor store to narrow down what type of gaiter will be best for you. For general use—trudging through the snow, hiking or snowshoeing—I suggest a high-cut gaiter with a Velcro closure and a tough rubber foot strap. Waterproof breathable material isn't necessary.

Sample Clothing List

When you've decided on materials and assembled all three layers of your winter clothing system, you should end up with something like this. This would be my minimum clothing list for a winter overnight trip in the mountains or the backcountry.

- Shell jacket (Gore-Tex or similar fabric).
- Shell pants (Gore-Tex or similar fabric).
- Down jacket, for extra warmth in camp or during breaks on the trail.
- Fleece jacket – for layering, or wearing under your shell jacket during the day.
- Long underwear top and bottom (synthetic or wool, never cotton), one set for the day and one set for night.
- Warm socks (wool/synthetic blend, never cotton), three pairs.
- Two pairs of warm gloves. One thin and one thick pair.
- Waterproof over-mitts (to keep your under-mitts/gloves dry. Wet mitts = cold hands).
- Warm hats (one with earflaps and some windproof capacity is best), two.

For a complete clothing packing list, see Appendix A.

Synthetic- or down-filled booties are a luxurious option for keeping your feet warm once you're at camp. Pack them away in a waterproof bag, and put them on when you change into your dry clothes and down jacket.

Sleeping Systems

Anticipating a warm and comfortable sleep can be all you need to get through the coldest or wettest of days. A good sleeping set-up will keep you warm when temperatures are well below freezing. The keys are the right equipment and, once again, layering.

The same principles used for layering clothing apply to layering for sleeping. You'll need to stay warm and dry from the outside in and from the inside out, and prevent perspiration from your body from building up inside your sleeping bag. Once again, the construction and materials of the equipment you choose play a crucial role in keeping you comfortable, and all have their pros and cons.

Basic Concepts

Many factors determine the insulating efficiency of your sleeping set-up. The better your sleeping set-up is, the less your body has to work at producing extra heat to keep you warm, and the less of your energy stores you will use up. Here are a few factors to consider when choosing a sleeping bag. (Note that many of these same principles apply to clothing as well.)

Dead air space is the extra space or room in a garment or sleeping bag between your body and the insulation. The more dead air space, the less efficient it will be at keeping you warm.

R-value refers to how efficient something is at insulating, and is a term used for everything from home construction materials to sleeping pads. The higher the number, the better a material is at insulating. For example, a 1/2-inch-thick (1 cm) closed-cell foam sleeping pad might have an R-value rating of 3, but a sleeping pad made of the same materials that is 3/4-inch-thick (1.5 cm) might have an R-value rating of 4.5.

Loft is the thickness of the bag when it's decompressed or fluffed up and full of air. You can measure the loft of a bag by spreading it on the floor and observing its thickness. The more loft a sleeping bag has, the warmer it will be. When buying a new bag, you'll often see the loft thickness recorded in inches or centimeters.

Bellows effect refers to how warm air can be pushed out of a garment or sleeping bag when you move.

Sleeping Bags

When choosing a sleeping bag, you'll want to consider how to minimize dead air space and bellows effect, and how to maximize R-value and loft—but without ending up with a bag that is so big that it fills your backpack. Let's start with a comparison of down and synthetic fill sleeping bags.

Down is such a good insulator because it traps warm air very effectively.

Down Fill Sleeping Bags

Down is the fluffy layer of insulating feathers, also known as plumules, found under a bird's exterior feathers. Down is very light and compressible, giving it the highest warmth-to-weight ratio of any insulating fill. The down used in sleeping bags and jackets usually comes from either ducks or geese.

When looking at the specifications for different down sleeping bags, look at the "fill power" or "loft power" of the down, which is a gauge of its quality and insulating efficiency. Fill power indicates the number of cubic inches of volume that one ounce of down displaces. The higher the fill power of the down, the less of it you need to keep warm; for example, you will need twice the weight of 400-fill down in a bag to keep you warm at 0°F (-18°C) than you would of 800-fill. Thus the lower the quality of the down, the heavier and bulkier it will be in comparison. Buyer beware: fill power measurements are not standardized, so one manufacturer's 700-fill may not be as high-quality as another's. When comparing sleeping bags, spread them out and measure the loft yourself.

Down Fill Power Ratings

400 to 450 fill: Lower quality, usually made from duck down.

500 to 600 fill: Medium quality, good price range, usually made from duck or goose down, or a mix.

650 to 800 fill: Excellent quality, almost always made of goose down, with the best warmth-to-weight ratio.

The bag on the left, rated to -40°F (-40°C), has a loft twice as high as the bag on the right which is rated 5°F (-15°C).

The beauty of down is that it has a high loft but can pack down relatively small.

Here's a summary of the advantages and disadvantages of down fill bags:

ADVANTAGES

- very comfortable
- very high warmth-to-weight and warmth-to-volume ratio
- will last a life time if properly cared for
- very compressible and compact

DISADVANTAGES

- significantly more expensive than a synthetic bag with the same temperature rating
- loses almost all of its insulating value when wet
- takes a very long time to dry; almost impossible to do without a dryer
- a hassle to clean

Synthetic Fill Sleeping Bags

Synthetic insulation, usually made from polyester fiber, is a petroleum byproduct—warmth from plastic. Most synthetic fill looks like cotton batting; it's a spider web of long extruded polyester threads crimped together into spongy sheets. There is no fill power to look for when choosing a synthetic sleeping bag, but there is the temperature rating of the bag to consider and the type of synthetic fill used. There are many different brands of synthetic fill—including Quallofil, Hollofil, Maxsoft, Thinsulate, Polarguard HV, Polarguard 3D, Polarguard Delta and PrimaLoft—each with different properties of durability, warmth, weight and bulk. Typically, there is a tradeoff to be made when choosing synthetic fills: the lightest and most compact synthetic materials tend to be the most expensive and the least durable, losing their loft over time.

Here's a summary of the advantages and disadvantages of synthetic fill bags:

ADVANTAGES

- very cost efficient, generally around 50% less than a down bag of the same temperature rating
- good in damp conditions; retains much of its insulating value even when soaking wet
- dries quickly in the field compared to down
- non-allergenic

DISADVANTAGES

- very bulky, harder to compress
- not as comfortable as down (doesn't conform to your body as well)
- short lifespan; loft and temperature rating diminish with use
- special care is required when packing and storing

In the down versus synthetic debate, there really is no right answer. To come up with your own solution, ask yourself the following questions and compare your answers to the pros and cons discussed above:

- How much am I willing to spend?
- Will I be doing a lot of camping with this bag in the near future? Or will it only really be used once or twice?

Always hang your sleeping bag or put it in a big garbage-bag-sized sack when storing it at home. This will allow the bag to stay lofted up, extending its life.

- Do I need a bag that is very light?
- Are size and compressibility priorities for me?
- Do I need a bag that will perform well in damp situations?

Sleeping Bag Shapes

As if choosing an insulating material wasn't enough, now you need to decide on the shape of your sleeping bag. There are three basic sleeping bag shapes to choose from, all of which have advantages and disadvantages. However, only one is the best for warmth.

Rectangular Bag

ADVANTAGES

- big
- lots of room to stretch
- might be big enough to fit a special someone inside with you!
- good for the summer

DISADVANTAGES

- loose fit means lots of dead air space that your body heat will have to warm up, making you colder
- lots of extra material adds weight and bulk
- not good for winter

Barrel Bag

ADVANTAGES

- more form-fitting than a rectangular bag; less dead air space
- width in the middle provides arm and leg room

DISADVANTAGES

- still lots of dead air space
- still has excess material, adding weight and bulk
- usually has no hood or neck yoke

Mummy Bag

ADVANTAGES

- warmest style of bag
- fits very snugly, eliminating most dead air space for maximum heating efficiency
- minimal use of material makes bag light and compressible
- usually includes an insulating hood
- usually includes a neck yoke and draw cord to prevent heat from escaping

DISADVANTAGES

- tight fit takes some getting used to
- not much extra space inside
- no room for friends

To sum up, if you want to be warm in the winter, buy yourself a mummy bag. It might feel a bit uncomfortable and claustrophobic at first, but I can guarantee that when you're all nice and warm on a cold winter's night, you'll be happy with your choice!

Sleeping Bag Features

After choosing a material and shape for your sleeping bag, make sure you have all the important features to keep you warm and comfortable.

1. Hood *This is a mandatory sleeping bag feature for winter camping and can add a lot of extra warmth with minimal extra weight. You will be amazed at how much warmer you will sleep just by pulling a nice fluffy hood over your head at night.*

2. Yoke *A yoke is a bit like a scarf on the inside of your sleeping bag, usually in the form of a puffy tube of insulation around the neck area. Sometimes there is a drawstring to secure it in a comfortable position. This internal scarf keeps you warmer by reducing heat loss through the bellows effect, which involves a combination of convection and radiation.*

3. Draft Tube *A draft tube is an extra sleeve of insulation that covers the zipper on the inside of your sleeping bag. This feature reduces heat loss through conduction (your warm skin in contact with a cold zipper), convection (a draft blowing through the zipper), and radiation (heat radiated through the tiny spaces of the zipper).*

4. Foot Box *The foot box is a roomy space at the end of the sleeping bag that is large enough for your feet to rest in a natural position without compressing the loft of the bag. It can be a great place to throw damp socks or boot liners. Chances are when you wake up in the morning, they will be dry and warm!*

Sleeping Bag Features (con't)

• **Dry Foot** Some sleeping bags come with a "dry foot" option, which incorporates a material with greater water resistance around the foot box—the area that most often touches the wet walls of your tent, tarp or snow shelter. A very popular material for this is Gore DryLoft, which is a special laminate that is bonded to the inside of the face fabric of some down sleeping bags. It is designed to keep outside moisture from seeping into your sleeping bag's insulation, but is also breathable, letting the moisture vapor from your body escape. DryLoft doesn't mean that your sleeping bag is waterproof; it's not. But this is a worthwhile feature if you can afford the extra cost. Having a DryLoft dry foot is more affordable than having DryLoft throughout the whole bag.

• **Construction** When comparing sleeping bags, pay attention to how they are constructed. There are different ways of sewing sleeping bags and the best ones prevent the insulation from moving around while ensuring that there are no seams or thin spots where heat can escape. Less expensive down bags will have sewn-through construction, meaning the seams go straight through the bag and create thin spots where heat can escape. High-quality down bags have baffled construction, with mesh dividers between sections to keep the down in place. Synthetic bags typically use "offset quilt" or "shingle" construction, the latter being the most energy efficient—and the most expensive.

Temperature Ratings

"How do I know if my sleeping bag will be warm enough?" Good question. Begin by estimating the coldest temperature that you might ever sleep in. All bags come with a temperature rating measured in degrees Fahrenheit and Celsius. But that doesn't mean that you can buy a bag rated for lower than your estimated coldest temperature and always be warm. The temperature rating of a bag is based on an average and includes a few assumptions: that you have some sort of barrier between you and the ground like a foam sleeping pad (minimizing heat loss through conduction); that you have some sort of shelter above and around you (minimizing heat loss through radiation and convection); that you are properly hydrated and nourished; and that you have an average metabolism. Any time you change one of these assumptions, you will be effectively changing the temperature rating of your sleeping bag.

Everyone has a different comfort level and some people just sleep warmer or colder than others. I have slept many nights out under the stars in my −4°F (−20°C) down bag in temperatures well below −4°F and have been comfortable. It will take a couple of nights out winter camping to discover how warm of a sleeper you are and the limitations of your sleeping bag.

Bring along a warm hat for sleeping, different than the sweaty one you wore all day, to keep that precious heat in at night. I have a hat that I use specifically for sleeping, made of 200-weight fleece with full ear coverage and a drawstring that I can cinch around my chin. If you find yourself a bit too warm, taking your hat off is an easy way to regulate body heat.

Overbags

An overbag is a very thin synthetic sleeping bag that can be used on its own in very warm temperatures (50–60°F, 10–15°C) but its primary use is as an extra layer to slip over your main synthetic or down bag. An overbag adds about 10–18°F (5–10°C) to your bag's temperature rating—and also serves the important function of keeping your sleeping bag dry.

Moisture is your enemy when you're sleeping out in the winter. You are continuously losing moisture from your body in the form of mostly invisible vapor. As soon as this vapor comes into contact with the cold, outside layer of your sleeping bag, it condenses into liquid and soaks into your bag's insulation. Moisture from your breath can also condense on the inside shelter walls and drip down onto you, seeping into your sleeping bag from the outside. If your sleeping bag is insulated with down, this moisture buildup will greatly reduce its warmth over time.

When you use an overbag, all of this moisture goes into the overbag instead; your sleeping bag stays dry. The overbag is relatively easy to dry out because it is thin and synthetic. This trick is especially useful for extended winter trips (two or more nights) when you are using a down sleeping bag. A good quality overbag costs between $80 and $130. Overbags are also available with DryLoft.

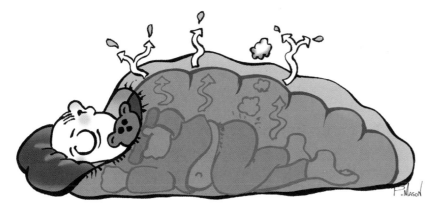

An overbag protects your sleeping bag from moisture as condensation will collect on the overbag instead.

Vapor-Barrier Liners (VBLs)

A vapor-barrier liner (VBL) is another way of dealing with the moisture that you give off when you sleep. First you slip into your VBL, then you slip into your sleeping bag. Usually made of polyurethane-coated or silicone-impregnated nylon, a VBL is designed to trap every ounce of moisture coming from your pores before it can enter your sleeping bag's insulation. This may sound uncomfortable, but it really isn't that bad. Your body can only reach 80% saturation, meaning that when it's surrounded by a certain amount of moisture it will not produce any more. So even if you slept in an actual garbage bag for a whole week, you would never be soaked, just damp.

And it works! By preventing any moisture from entering into your sleeping bag from the inside, you can ensure that the loft of your bag stays at almost 100% for the duration of your trip—as long as it's also protected from outside moisture. A VBL adds up to 10–18°F (5–10°C) of warmth to your sleeping system with a minimal increase in weight and bulk.

If you choose to sleep in a VBL, wear a base layer of thin long-sleeve tops and bottoms next to your skin. You already know that the first layer in the layering system is designed to keep your skin dry, so you won't really feel the dampness. In the morning, you will be warmer and more comfortable when you crawl out of your bag. Radiating heat from your body will dry out your next-to-skin layer in minutes through convection. Turn your VBL inside out, put it outside to let the cold air freeze the built-up moisture, give it a shake and voilà! Your VBL is dry and ready to pack up.

Fleece and Silk Liners

Another great and inexpensive option that you can add to your sleep layering system is a fleece liner. A fleece liner will add another 10°F (5°C) or more to your sleeping system and only costs about $30 to $50. You can get fleece liners with a full zipper and a hood, or opt out of these bells and whistles and pay a lot less. Of course, if you are good with the sewing machine, buy a sheet of fleece, sew yourself a fleece liner and customize it however you like.

Adding a silk or even a thin cotton liner will add a bit more comfort to your sleeping system, but the real benefit of a thin liner like this is that it traps all of the oil, sweat and dirt from your body—meaning you'll have to wash your sleeping bag less often, which is less wear and tear on your sleeping bag and less work for you. Simply remove the liner after every trip, throw it in the washer and your sleeping bag is clean!

Sleeping Pads

Your sleeping bag doesn't reach its full temperature rating potential without a sleeping pad. You need something between your body and the ground or most of your core heat will be sucked away through conduction. And, what do you know, there are options in this category too! Both open- and closed-cell foam sleeping pads come in a variety of different thicknesses. The thinner the pad, the lower the R-value; the thicker the pad, the higher the R-value.

Open-cell Foam Pads

Open-cell foam pads are similar to a sponge: soft, squishy and full of air bubbles or pockets. Open-cell foam construction is mostly used in self-inflating sleeping pads with

Weather permitting, bring your sleeping bag out of your shelter and hang it from a tree before you make breakfast. The moisture will evaporate or, if it's cold out, will freeze and can be brushed off.

an airtight, nylon shell like those made by Therm-a-Rest. You can blow a bit of air into them to reach your desired firmness, then close the valve and lie down to sleep.

ADVANTAGES:

- very comfortable
- compact
- lightweight
- can be folded into a camp chair if you get a chair kit

DISADVANTAGES:

- expensive
- not as durable, can be punctured (and repaired)
- not the warmest option for winter camping

Closed-cell Foam Pads

Closed-cell foam is firm with no compressible air pockets or holes. This tried and true style of sleeping pad has been around the longest. There are a variety of closed-cell pads, but for the most part they are very similar and your decision will come down to thickness, weight and comfort. Your choices are essentially between the standard "blue foamy", the yellow Evazote, and the "egg carton" style that has a ridged surface. Personally, I prefer the Evazote pad because in my experience it is the most durable, absorbs less moisture (almost none) and remains the most malleable at much colder

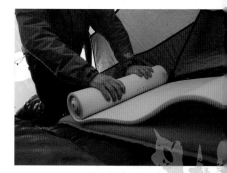

If you have the room you can always bring both types of pad. Simply ensure you keep the closed-cell pad closest to your body so you don't use your body heat to warm the air pockets of the open-cell pad.

temperatures (-94°F, -70°C). However, some of my friends prefer the ridged-surface pads because they find them more comfortable than most other closed-cell pads.

ADVANTAGES:

- less expensive than open-cell pads
- very durable
- light
- can be used for many different things
- excellent R value in all four seasons
- can't go flat on you

DISADVANTAGES:

- bulkier
- less comfortable than self-inflating open-cell foam pads

Other Types of Pads

In addition to the two basic types—open-cell and closed-cell pads—there are some combos and alternatives out there. Therm-a-Rest makes combination pads that have closed-cell foam on the bottom and self-inflating open-cell foam on top. These pads combine the comfort and compactness of open-cell with the puncture-resistance and reliability of closed-cell. You can also find inflatable mattresses filled with a variety of insulating materials. One type, filled with down and called a DownMat, has a very high R-value.

Decisions, Decisions

In this chapter we have discussed many options for clothing layers, sleeping systems, insulating materials and more. As you outfit yourself with these things, you may feel overwhelmed by all the choices you have to make. You will find yourself juggling trade-offs such as lightweight versus bombproof, feature-loaded versus more affordable, waterproof versus highly breathable. There are no magically correct answers to any of these decisions because every individual's needs are slightly different.

Don't despair! Try to have fun creating a system that works best for you, and have fun tweaking things until you get the perfect combination. Take your own ideals and philosophies into account and decide what combination will work best for you and your overall objectives.

If you take some time and choose your gear and clothing carefully, your reward will be clothing and sleeping layering systems that will work in any weather, in any season, and keep you warm, dry and comfortable on many fun adventures!

Closed-cell foam pads can be used for more than just sleeping: making splints, insulating water bottles, standing on while cooking dinner, and marking out a checkerboard.

COOKING & EATING

No matter how hard a day you've had, how bad the weather, how cold or wet you get, or even how tired, a good meal can turn everything around. Food is also critical for giving your body the fuel it needs to move and stay warm. It'll pay off hugely to bring and eat lots of good food on your winter backpacking trip.

Chapter 2

Winter Nutrition

Creating a Trip Menu

Packing Your Food

Stoves

Winter Nutrition

Eating a well-planned and balanced diet while winter backpacking will improve your physical health, your state of mind, your energy level, your performance, and keep you warm. Putting food into your body is like putting wood on a fire. Both food and heat energy can be measured in calories. The more wood you throw onto the fire, the longer and hotter it will burn. But just as there are many different kinds of wood, which are best used for different purposes, there are also different types of food energy.

Macronutrients

Macronutrients are the basic building blocks of food energy. They also include vitamins and minerals, which do not provide energy but perform important functions through-out the body. If you have a well balanced diet, you will get all the vitamins and minerals you need.

There are three main sources of macronutrients: carbohydrate, fat and protein. A good winter camping diet includes all three in these specific proportions: 65%, 20% and 15%, but just use this as a guideline—you don't have to measure everything out!

Of course, only a few foods are entirely made of one of these things, so you have to look at what something is mostly made of. For example, while nuts are primarily a good source of healthy fats, they are also very high in protein and are partly carbohydrate.

Carbohydrate: 65%

Carbohydrates, or "carbs," should make up the biggest proportion of your diet. There are two basic types—simple carbs and complex carbs—and your winter food plan should contain a mix of both.

Simple carbs are the first thing the body converts to energy and also the first to be used up. You can think of them as a piece of dry cedar thrown on a fire; it will flare up almost instantly and give off lots of heat, but will burn out very quickly.

Complex carbs are used more slowly by your body, but will also be used up fairly quickly when you are active, so you need to keep fuelling your body continually throughout the day. Complex carbohydrates typically contain both starch and fibre. Fibre can actually increase satiety (the feeling of being full) and slows down the release of energy. (It also keeps you regular!)

Your breakfast, lunch and snacks throughout the day should consist mostly of simple and complex carbs. A great example of a meal that includes both kinds of carbs is a big bowl of oatmeal (complex) for breakfast with a sprinkle of brown sugar (simple), some rehydrated apples (mostly complex) and some raisins (mostly simple).

Granola and nut bars are great snacks because they combine grains (complex carbs) and nuts (fat, protein and carbs), with sugars (simple carbs) to provide both quick and lasting energy

Examples of Simple and Complex Carbohydrates

SIMPLE CARBOHYDRATES	COMPLEX CARBOHYDRATES
Glucose (dextrose)	Grains
Table sugar (sucrose)	Fruits
Honey (fructose and glucose)	Potatoes
Fructose (sugars in fruit)	Pasta
Maltose (sugars in malt)	Macaroni
Lactose (sugars in milk)	Seaweed
Brown sugar	Algae
Corn syrup	Peas
Maple syrup	Beans (Legumes)
Refined sugar products	Veggies
Raw sugar	Brown Rice
Molasses	Lentils
Candies	

Fat: 20%

Fat, another of the macronutrients, serves many important functions: adds taste; satisfies the sense of hunger; insulates the body; protects organs; stores energy; and helps to transport various minerals and nutrients to different parts of the body.

Fat is the most concentrated form of food energy there is—more than twice the calories per weight than carbs or protein—so it forms a larger part of a winter backpacking diet than it does in an everyday diet.

So why not just fill your pack with fatty food to save weight and meet all your caloric requirements that way? Because your body does not metabolize fat into readily available energy right away. For example, if you eat a highly fatty breakfast, you will feel sluggish all morning until your body has finally metabolized the fat. Eating fat is like throwing a piece of oak on the fire—it burns hot and slow, and you wouldn't use it to start a fire! You should eat most of your fats toward the end of the day or before bed when you are expending less energy.

Load up on fats in the evening to keep you sleeping warmer all night long. One great way is by adding a dollop of butter to your evening hot chocolate-but remember you can only get away with this on trip!

There are fats to use in moderation and there are good, healthy sources of fat that should make up the bulk of your fat intake.

• *Saturated Fats* Fats to limit are the saturated fats that are generally found in animal foods. These contain a lot of energy but they also increase the risk of heart disease. Sources of saturated fats include red meat, butter, lard, chicken skin, whole milk dairy products, palm oil and coconut oil. Most of these fats can be identified by the fact that they are solid at room temperature.

• *Monounsaturated, Polyunsaturated and Omega-3 Fats* Emphasize these healthier fats, which include most vegetable oils and the fats in avocados, nuts and seeds. Omega-3 fat—a type of polyunsaturated fat that your body needs to function well, and which protects against heart disease—is found in fatty fish (salmon, mackerel, sardines, rainbow trout), flax oil and ground flax seeds.

So for example, eating nut butter sandwiches or tinned fish at lunch will provide you with some fat, but also with needed protein.

Protein: 15%

Protein is a macronutrient that provides some energy for the body, but energy is not its main function. Protein builds muscle, repairs injuries, and supports other essential functions.

Protein is made up of several amino acids. There are about 20 amino acids and nine of them are called "essential amino acids." Your body cannot make these nine essential amino acids; you need to get them from your diet by eating protein. Good sources of protein include eggs, legumes (like lentils and chick peas), lean meats, fish, poultry, dairy products and soy products like tofu.

How Much Energy Do You Need?

You can estimate how much food to bring by calculating your caloric requirements, and then packing food to meet that requirement. The food energy of various macronutrients is as follows:

Carbohydrates = 4 calories per gram

Fats = 9 calories per gram

Proteins = 4 calories per gram

There are a few different calculations out there that will help to give you an idea of how many calories you should consume every 24 hours, depending on your level of activity. Gender, individual metabolism and level of fitness also make a difference and vary from person to person, so this is only a guideline.

Resting Energy Expenditure (REE)

You can begin by calculating your resting energy expenditure, or REE. This is the

GORP stands for "Good Old Raisins and Peanuts" but includes any kind of trail mix, including ones with chocolate! They offer a perfect combination of fats and proteins when you are on the go and can be adapted to match anyone's taste.

amount of energy you need to survive. This may also be referred to as basal metabolism—a couch potato's energy needs.

Age 18 to 30: 6.95 x weight + 679

Age 30 to 60: 5.27 x weight + 679

Example:

Ben Shillington weighs 160 lbs, so his REE is 6.95 x 160 + 679 = 1,791 calories per day.

Total Energy Expenditure

Your total energy expenditure combines your REE with your activity level to determine the total amount of energy (calories) you will need each day. You calculate it by multiplying your REE by an "activity factor" of 1.3 to 2.4, depending on what activity you are doing. Use the chart below to calculate your activity factor.

Trudging through the snow takes a lot more out of you than just regular hiking. Be sure to consider this when calculating your caloric needs.

Another non-meat source of protein is something called texturized vegetable protein (TVP). While TVP might not sound very appetizing, it's a great supplement for vegetarians in your group. It's fairly bland, and like chicken it tends to take on the flavours of whatever else you're cooking it with. It's also dry and reconstitutes quickly.

ENERGY LEVEL	EXAMPLE		ACTIVITY FACTOR
Very light	Reading a book or watching Oprah		1.3
Light	Light walk		1.6
Moderate	Light jog		1.7
Heavy	Swimming laps		2.1
Exceptional	Winter expedition		2.4

Example:

Ben Shillington on a winter expedition burns 1,791 calories x 2.4 (activity factor) = 4,298 calories/day, plus a few extra calories for really cold temperatures.

Ben's total energy expenditure = 4,500 calories/day.

The most important thing to note is that winter travel consumes more than twice the calories of everyday activities at home. Food is fuel, and you will be burning lots of fuel to travel and stay warm.

Fueling the Fire All Day Long

When winter backpacking, you should try to eat an average of 65% carbs, 20% fat and 15% protein during a given day, but for individual meals the proportions are a little different. Here's how the macronutrient mix plays out through your winter's day for optimum performance.

Breakfast

Your breakfast should consist mostly of simple and complex carbs to give you quick energy right off the bat. You should be consuming at least 500 of your daily caloric intake at breakfast, and up to 1,000 if possible. See the *Winter Breakfast Ideas* section for meal suggestions.

Lunch

I call lunch an "all-day meal" because lunch should really consist of grazing throughout the day and not necessarily be a specific meal. Snacking all day will allow you to constantly supply your body with the fuel it needs while on the go. This will also prevent you from having to stop for a long lunch session where you might overstuff yourself or even get a little chilly from reduced activity. Depending on your specific personal requirements, try to consume 1,500 to 2,000 calories throughout the day in the form of snacks and lunch foods. It may help to consume some of these calories—about 500—in the form of liquids like soup, hot drinks, and diluted energy drinks and juices. Drinking fluid calories reduces the amount you need to eat while helping to keep you hydrated. See the *Winter Lunch Ideas* section for meal suggestions.

Dinner

If you're camping out, dinner is when you can pack in your remaining 1,500-plus daily calories. This is a great time to incorporate more protein to feed and repair your muscles, and fat to set your internal furnace on a slow burn for the night. Pastas, rich sauces,

Pancakes with plenty of syrup offer an excellent combination of simple and complex carbohydrates.

Vegetarian goulash is a hearty meal that is both filling and warm.

meats, nuts and meals that incorporate oil are some good choices for dinner. See the *Winter Dinner Ideas* section for meal suggestions.

Hydration

You may not think of winter as a sweaty time, but the fact is that your body loses a lot of water in the winter just through breathing in cold, dry air and breathing out hot, moist air. More is lost through perspiration, urination, and digestion of all that extra food, so staying hydrated is especially important.

On average you can loose up to 4 cups (1L) of water an hour when engaged in moderate to heavy output activities. You should sip water, juice, hot drinks or soup throughout the day to replace this loss. Your body can absorb about 3 cups (750 ml) of water an hour, but you can make up the difference by drinking more when you're in camp. It's also a good idea to start consuming extra water a day or two before you leave on a winter camping trip to ensure that you are "topped up" once you head out.

What you drink is not as important as how much you drink. You may have heard that coffee and tea are no good because caffeine dehydrates you, but this is not true, particularly when you are active. You are still getting lots of fluid into your body and coffee is only a diuretic when used at rest. Energy drinks and juices are best diluted by half, because very sweet drinks are not absorbed as well by the body.

If you find that you are really thirsty, this is a bad sign, as you are already on your way to dehydrating. A guideline I like to use is the "3 quart rule." Between breakfast and dinner you should have consumed 3 quarts (3L) of water in some form or another throughout

the day. If you can get another half to full quart in after dinner, it's even better. Proper hydration will also help you to stay warm and will provide you with more energy. You need water to keep your blood thin enough to circulate efficiently throughout your body and to aid in digestion of food. Food equals calories and calories equal energy and heat.

If you are peeing frequently and your pee is clear, that means you adequately hydrated and should be feeling pretty good. If your pee is a yellow or even orange, that's a bad sign and you really need to increase your fluid intake. I've found that a bonus of peeing, especially if you're feeling cold, is that you almost instantly start to warm up because your body is no longer wasting energy to keep the pee warm.

Convenience is sometimes the key to staying adequately hydrated. If you have a backpack with a water bottle pocket on the side, this is a great spot to store your bottle so you can drink on the fly. If you don't, store it in the top pocket of your pack so it's easy to have a buddy grab it for you.

There are many reasons why people don't drink enough in the winter. Be aware of these so they don't happen to you:

- Thinking that because it's cold, you won't get thirsty or sweat.
- Wanting to avoid having to pee in the cold.
- Letting your water bottle freeze or your hydration bag and hose freeze.
- Packing water where it is inaccessible and not wanting to stop and take it out.
- Failing to prepare water in the morning or the night before camping.

Types of Water Bottles

The best kind of water bottle to have for winter camping is a plastic water bottle with a wide mouth. I like to use 1-quart (1 L) Nalgene bottles. A wide-mouth bottle is easier to fill without spilling and less likely to freeze around the opening—and if it does freeze, it's easier to chip the ice out or melt it with boiling water. These bottles also seal very reliably so they won't leak, and in my experience they are almost indestructible.

There's one potential problem with plastic bottles and you might want to be careful about what your bottle is made of. Recent studies have shown that polycarbonate plastic bottles—the most popular kind of water bottle made of a hard, see-through plastic—can leach a potentially dangerous chemical called Bisphenol-A (BPA). The problem is worse if you're filling the bottle with hot or boiling water, which in the winter you'll be doing frequently. These studies have generated a lot of controversy about what people can safely use when camping, and in making a decision about what type of water bottle to use, I recommend that you do your own research.

The safer alternative seems to be the older-style Nalgene bottles that are made of a soft, opaque plastic called high-density polyethylene (HDPE). This type of plastic has been around for a long time and isn't known to leach anything dangerous into the water. There's also a new type of plastic called Tritan, available in bottles from CamelBak and GSI Outdoors, that is BPA-free and supposedly safer at high temperatures.

If you don't want to take a risk on any kind of plastic, you can use stainless steel or aluminum bottles. But keep in mind that metal conducts heat and cold; it's more likely to freeze to your lips if it's cold or burn you if it's hot. And metal bottles usually have smaller openings that freeze more quickly.

In the winter, I don't recommend using a hydration bladder system, however convenient it may seem; these always freeze, starting with the hose, and sometimes burst and soak gear. It's also difficult to pour water into a hydration bag without spilling.

To keep any type of water bottle from freezing, you can buy foam insulating sleeves, make one out of closed-cell foam and duct tape, or use a sock. (An insulating sleeve

Pour a little water in the bottom of the pot before adding snow in order to avoid a burnt flavor and a ruined pot.

Store your water bottle upside-down (making sure that it is properly sealed). Water always freezes from the top first, so this will ensure that your lid won't freeze shut and there will be liquid to drink and not a layer of ice.

will be especially important if you choose to use metal water bottles, since reducing the metal's conductivity will protect your skin from extreme heat and cold, and help insulate the contents better.) During the day you can carry your water bottle on a strap inside your jacket or fleece to keep it warm and easy to access. At night, store your water bottles in your sleeping bag—just make sure the lids are screwed on very, very tightly!

Getting and Purifying Water

For day trips, it's easy to head out fully stocked with water, but if you're out on a camping trip, evening is usually the best time to restock your supply. Unless there are open bodies of water or unfrozen streams nearby, your water will likely come from melting snow or ice. Melting snow to get water is time-consuming and not very efficient—a 1-quart (1L) pot of snow will melt down to about a quarter-cup of water—but you often have no choice when winter camping.

When melting snow, you need to be careful not to burn the snow! It sounds funny, but you can actually burn snow, and it tastes awful. If you fill up your pot with snow and toss it on the stove, heat gets trapped between the snow and the bottom of the pot and burns the pot, imparting the flavor to the snow. The trick is to add a little bit of water to the bottom of the pot first and let it heat up a bit, then slowly add snow until you have a sufficient volume of warm water to fill the rest of the pot with snow. While you're melting snow, try to take the lid off the pot as little as possible; just be patient. It will save time and fuel to keep the lid on.

No matter how you get your water, boiling is the best way to purify it when winter camping. Purification pumps, which are fantastic for summer camping, are useless in cold weather because they freeze easily and are very likely to crack and be ruined. Since you are usually melting snow on your stove anyway, it is not much extra work to bring it to a boil.

Creating a Trip Menu

One of the most challenging and important things about heading out on any multi-day trip is planning the menu and then packing it. You want to ensure that you are going to have enough food for everyone. It's nice to have a variety of food but you also need to cut down on bulk and weight. It's a lot to think about, especially if you're packing food for a group, but it's not so hard if you proceed methodically. Here are the basic steps to create a menu.

- Start out by making yourself a menu chart and figuring out how many breakfasts, lunches, dinners, snacks and desserts you need for the whole trip.

- Fill in each meal with things you'd like to eat, including ingredients and recipes if applicable.

Example: Breakfast Day 2

1¾ cups granola

¼ cup powdered whole milk

1 cup dehydrated apple

1 tbsp peanut butter

1 apple-mango tea bag

- Try to follow the macronutrient proportions we discussed for the whole day (65% carbs, 15% protein, 20% fat) as well as for each meal (high-carb breakfasts and lunches, fats and proteins at dinner) as best you can.

- Evaluate potential meals based on which ingredients are the easiest to pack and best suited for winter. Remember that any moisture-containing foods will freeze, which can be both an advantage and a disadvantage: you can pack fresh meats and fish (pack them frozen and they will stay frozen), but things like fresh fruit and veggies will be ruined. Fruits and veggies work the best in the winter if they are dehydrated. Often adding dehydrated fruit to hot oatmeal, or veggies and meat to a soup or sauce, is all that is needed to reconstitute them. You can dehydrate food yourself with a dehydrator or buy it at a grocery or bulk food store.

- There are also a lot of great camping cookbooks out there that are full of good meal ideas. Even though most are written for spring, summer and fall camping, many recipes are just fine for winter camping too, or can be made suitable with some minor adjustments. I like the one put out by Black Feather, a renowned outfitter in Canada that leads trips and expeditions all over the north. There's also a good one by NOLS.

- Calculate the quantities and servings needed per meal, keeping in mind the number of calories you need based on your total energy expenditure.

- Make a grocery list of all the ingredients you will need to purchase, translating them where possible into the packaged quantities available at the grocery store. This will make your shopping at the grocery store easier.

Example:

8 cups (32 oz / 900 g) of whole wheat penne noodles = 2 x 16 oz. (450 g) bags

6 packages instant oatmeal mixed flavors = 1 box Quaker variety pack

It helps to do a quick walk around a grocery store or two to see what is available and how much things cost before making your menu and grocery list.

Sample Winter Meals

Everyone has their own tastes and preferences. Some like lots of variety and enjoy preparing a gourmet meal. Others can eat the same thing every day and can't be bothered to spend an hour preparing something that's going to get devoured in minutes. No

If you are planning on using something like dehydrated hamburger meat for your dinner, you can save some time and fuel by adding some hot water to your burger midday and then sealing it up in its Ziploc bag. Store the burger in the top pouch of your backpack so it won't get squished. By dinnertime, your hamburger will be well reconstituted and will cook in minutes!

matter what your tendency, winter is a fine time to slip into the latter category and be happy with something that is filling, warm, quick and easy to cook, and minimizes fuel consumption. You'll find yourself wanting to use the fewest dishes possible to prepare. In winter, you do not wash dishes as you traditionally would. Instead, simply boil water in a dirty pot and drink it to get the extra calories, or scour remaining food particles out with a bit of snow.

Winter Breakfast Ideas

Breakfasts in the winter can be simple, easy quick and tasty, and you can ensure a variety if that is what you need. If you are planning on being on the move soon after breakfast, you can simplify your first meal of the day by sticking to something like instant oatmeal so you don't have to dirty a pot. Remember your breakfast should consist mostly of carbohydrates, both simple and complex.

- granola with powdered skim milk
- instant flavored oatmeal packages
- bulk oatmeal with sugar, dried fruit and peanut butter

Dehydrated food, such as dried fruit, can sometimes be consumed as-is, or it can be reconstituted.

- any kind of hot or cold cereal with powdered milk and dried fruit
- bagel with cream cheese and jam

You can augment these items or any others that you may pack with the following.
- dehydrated fruit pieces
- fruit leather
- cereal bars
- mixed nuts
- coffee/tea/hot chocolate

Winter Lunch Ideas

Try to have a variety of snackable items that you can munch on throughout the day to give yourself a continuous flow of energy. Like breakfast, lunch will consist mostly of carbs, though you can throw in some meat, cheese and nuts for variety and long-burning energy. Lunch should also not require much cooking, besides maybe heating up water for a hot drink or instant soup in your mug. Here are some ideas.
- Pre-made bagels and cream cheese (or any spread you desire)
- pre-made, individually packaged tortilla wraps
- granola or cereal bars
- instant soup (if you have the fuel and the time)
- fruit leather
- GORP
- crackers
- dried fruit
- candies
- rice cakes
- cheese cubes
- beef jerky
- pepperoni or salami sticks or your favorite deli meats

Winter Dinner Ideas

Dinner is a great time to stoke up the oven—your body's oven, that is. It's best to stick to a one-pot meal for simple prep and cleanup. If you only have one stove and need to heat up two pots, you might have a hard time keeping one warm while you are cooking the other. Remember, now is the best time to load up on your fats and proteins. Here are some suggestions.
- Pasta with garlic, pepper, parmesan cheese, olive oil and sliced pepperoni.
- Pasta noodles and any kind of sauce with pepperoni or frozen or dehydrated meat. I recommend powdered sauce packages from the grocery store that you add to water and oil. If you need to add milk, use powdered milk. Top it with cheese to get some tasty fats and proteins in you.

Slow-Cooked Bagels
Pre-cut, dress and bag the bagel at home. Insert individually-bagged frozen bagel into sock and add to toe box of sleeping bag at least 90 minutes prior to getting out of the tent. You can also cook in sleeping bag on low overnight. Once coffee is poured, unwrap bagel and consume.

If you have a food dehydrator and have used it to prepare meals for camping trips in summer, you might already know how easy it is to make and dehydrate some tomato sauces, chilies and stews to bring along. Then all you have to do is add hot water, stir or simmer for a few minutes, and enjoy with some noodles or rice, which also only take a few moments to prepare! Tomato-based sauces tend to rehydrate the best, but other legume-based recipes, like dahl, work well too. To adjust a recipe for dehydrating, make sure that chunks of things are chopped a little smaller than you'd do it if you were cooking at home, or even give your concoction a brief whirl in the blender. These will dehydrate faster and rehydrate more evenly and quickly too.

- Instant rice and dehydrated vegetable flakes and pepper, also with cheese.
- Instant rice with beans, with instant soup for flavor.
- Instant mashed potatoes with cheese.
- Canned sardines or smoked herring (great protein source at the end of the day).
- Noodle, rice, soup or potato packages. These come in a variety of flavors with all the ingredients and sauces needed and only take about 10 minutes to cook. If the instructions call for milk and butter, you can use powdered milk and small pre-packaged restaurant butter packages. Add a can of tuna to any of these prepackaged dinners for protein.

You can also purchase ready-made, freeze-dried meals that are quite tasty from companies such as Harvest Foodworks, Backpackers Pantry, Natural High and Mountain House. They are usually sold in "two-serving" packages, but beware that most will feed only one person with a large appetite. These are very convenient—often all you need to do is pour boiling water into the meal package itself, close the top and let it sit to cook. The disadvantage is that they can be more expensive than if you make your own food.

Some Favorite Recipes

Here are a few of my favorite recipes that I make frequently when I'm on winter camping trips. Enjoy!

Ben's Breakfast

I almost always pack the same breakfast for all of my winter trips and never get bored.

2 packages maple & brown sugar instant oatmeal

1 sliced dehydrated banana

1 sliced dehydrated apple

2 peanut butter balls (recipe below; usually added to the oatmeal)

1 delicious cup of strong, black, dark roast coffee

Bring water to a boil. Dump instant oatmeal and dried fruit in a bowl and then stir in the hot water. Set it aside to thicken while you make some coffee (I use a one-cup filter device). Only a few minutes after pouring the hot water, the oatmeal is ready to eat and the coffee is strong enough to drink. Throw in a couple of peanut butter balls before you dig into the oatmeal, and this breakfast will be sure to keep you going all day.

Make Your Own Meal Packages

Over that past few years I have become a big fan of what I like to call the "One-Man-Milk-Bag Meal." This is a meal that produces no dirty dishes, no garbage, takes only a few minutes to make, and gives you a hot drink and toasty warm hands as a bonus!

I buy my milk in 1-gallon (4 L) bags that come divided into three thick plastic bags that are each the perfect size for one of these instant dinner packages. If you don't buy milk this way, any heavy duty 1-quart (1 L) plastic bag will do.

1 ½ cups of instant white rice
¼ cup dehydrated vegetables (lots of onions and garlic is good)
1 beef or chicken bouillon cube
½ tsp of white flour
dash of salt and pepper
¼ cup dehydrated beef, chicken or textured vegetable protein (TVP)

Add all the ingredients to the bag, shake them up, squeeze out the air, and twist the bag closed. Seal it with a rubber band and it's ready to pack.

Cooking directions: Boil 4 cups (1L) of water. Open the milk bag and add about two cups (500 ml) of the hot water, or more if it looks like it's needed. Twist and reseal the bag with the rubber band. Put the hot bag inside your jacket for about eight minutes.

Meanwhile, pour the rest of the boiled water into your mug for hot chocolate or tea. Remove milk bag from jacket, open and add any extra seasonings, butter or oil, and eat. When finished, fold the milk bag and pack it out to clean when you get home and reuse on your next trip.

You can also put all the ingredients into a thermos in the morning and fill it with water. When it's time for lunch you'll have a thick and tasty hot soup. For this method, you can use normal rice instead of instant because it will be in the hot water long enough to cook. You can also put in any type of pasta noodle and it will be edible by lunchtime.

Shillington Fat Bars

This is one of my favorite winter snacks and many people find it completely disgusting as a concept until they taste it. This recipe also completely flies in the face of everything I just told you about healthy and unhealthy fats—it's full of the worst kinds.

Bring a paper coffee filter or cheesecloth to filter the bits of leaves, needles and bark out of your melted-snow water when you pour it into a bottle. That's what I call camp spice!

I excuse myself by explaining that I made up this recipe when I was 18, heading into the Adirondack Mountains for the first time to climb Mount Algonquin and Mount Marcy. I needed something to keep me going—and these babies certainly did.

Even though you'd probably die of a heart attack at age 30 if you ate like this all the time, once in a while can't be too bad for you, right? I still love this recipe because it is guaranteed to fill you up and keep you warm. Keep a chunk of these bad boys beside you when you're sleeping and have a bite or two if you wake up in the middle of the night to keep your internal furnace burning. You'll also find you're full of energy the next day. *Warning:* This snack is only to be consumed when you are in camp for the night. Do not consume if you plan on moving within four hours because you need time to digest these, like a python.

1 lb block of lard
1 lb block of butter
1 medium jar of your favorite peanut butter
1 cup bacon grease
½ cup chocolate chips
1 cup granola or coconut to hold 'er all together

Combine all the ingredients in one large pot and melt on medium heat. Once everything has blended together into a delicious stew of fatty warmth, pour it onto a big baking sheet and put it outside in the cold or into the fridge until it solidifies. Then cut into snack-size squares and individually wrap them with aluminum foil or plastic wrap.

Vegetarians can try replacing lard, butter and bacon grease with additional peanut butter and vegetable fats of your choice: margarine, shortening and coconut cream.

Peanut Butter Balls

This is an easy but sticky and messy recipe, which is less messy when kept cold. Fortunately, winter usually provides that part. These little peanut butter balls are terrific high-calorie snacks, full of simple sugar for energy, but also some complex carbs, protein, and plenty of fat for a more sustaining fuel when you want to stay warm.

1 medium or large container of your favorite peanut butter
Some delicious icing sugar
Chocolate chips
Some oatmeal or granola (for texture and to help bond the peanut butter molecules)
...And if you want to get fancy, toss in a bit a dried coconut

In a mixing bowl, slop in a few big scoops of your favorite peanut butter. Add two good sized handfuls of chocolate chips. Add one handful of texture and bonding agent of your choice. Lightly sprinkle an even coating of delicious icing sugar to eliminate some of the stickiness and add some flavor. (When I say sprinkle, I mean half a cup or so!) Finally, if you're a big gourmet,

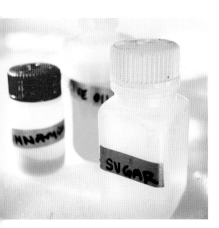

add a handful of dried coconut (which will also act as a texture and bonding agent).

Combine all ingredients and mix them together well using your clean hands, adding more icing sugar as needed to keep your hands a little less sticky. Cover a plate or area on your counter with icing sugar and coconut. Drop a teaspoon of the peanut butter mixture on top, make one at a time. Do your best to roll them into bite-sized balls. Place balls in a container or on a piece of wax paper and put them into the freezer. Once the balls are solid, pack them in small sealable bags, and leave stored in the freezer until the morning you leave.

As a variation, you can melt chocolate in the microwave and dip each ball in it before setting them in the freezer.

Packing Your Food

Food packing for multi-day trips is all about organization. The more organized you are, the easier and better your winter camping experience will be. It's better to take lots of time organizing and packing in the comfort of your home than to deal with the consequences of poor organization in the field when you're cold, tired and hungry. Now that you've sketched out your menu plan and shopped for your meal ingredients, you can begin to prep and pack your food by following these steps.

1. Remove and discard any unnecessary or excessive packaging, like boxes containing things that are individually wrapped or can be more efficiently packed in bags. This will help considerably in reducing weight, bulk and the amount of garbage you'll have to pack out. If you need any cooking instructions or nutritional information off the packages, just cut them out and keep them with the food.

2. Measure out the quantities of each ingredient for each meal. I suggest packing all of one meal group at a time: start with all the breakfasts, followed by lunches then dinners. Do any preparation of ingredients that's easier to do now than in the field when things will be frozen solid; for example, slice or cube cheeses and meats such as salami and pepperoni; grate your cheese if you want to add it to a pasta or rice dish.

3. Separate ingredients if needed into their own clear Ziploc baggie and then place every item for that one meal into one large Ziploc bag. Using a permanent marker, write the day, meal, and number of servings on the outside of the bag. You can also write down the caloric value per serving. For example: Day 2 breakfast, 2 servings, 1,420 calories.

4. Once you have all of your meals individually packed, lay them out on the kitchen table or the living room floor and group them into your meal plan days. This is a great way to make sure that you have not missed any meals and make any final changes to your menu. If you have recorded the caloric value of each meal on the front of your meal bags, you can calculate the total day's caloric value and make sure that you are close enough to your total energy expenditure.

If you have a different colored stuff sack for each meal (breakfasts, lunches and dinners) it will be easy to tell them apart. A duct tape label on the outside of each stuff sack is another way to identify what's inside.

5. *Your last step is to pack all of your meals.* If I'm going out on a short trip of two or three days, I just put all of my individually packed meals into one stuff sack. I have a bright red one that I always use for my food. For longer trips, you might want to separate your meals into three different stuff sacks—one each for breakfast, lunch and dinner. Or you may want to have one stuff sack per day with all meals and snacks for that day inside. If the stuff sacks are different colors it will be easy to tell them apart. A duct tape label on the outside of each stuff sack is another way to identify what's inside. No matter how you pack your food, you want a system that is quick and easy. When I am packing my bag each morning I like to pull out my lunch Ziploc for that day, put some of the food in my pockets for snacking and the rest in the top of my pack lid. That way when I stop for lunch, I don't have to open my pack.

Stoves

A hot campfire is a great source of warmth, a way to dry off, and a good spot to hang out and socialize. It can also take away the sense of loneliness when you're on your own, and can magically captivate you for hours and bring back fond memories. Fuel stoves don't

If you've never used your stove before, practice setting up and lighting it a couple of times at home (outside, of course). Even if you're familiar with your stove, you should test it before you go out.

do any of these things but they do offer many of their own comforts and advantages: you can have hot food and drink quickly wherever and whenever you want it; you can cook efficiently in any weather; you don't have to gather wood; and, done properly, you can even cook in the comfort of your tent by putting your stove in the vestibule. In the spring, summer and fall, you can get away without using a stove. But in the winter, a stove is critical to your survival, enjoyment and comfort.

Liquid Fuel Stoves

The best choice of stove for winter camping is the liquid fuel stove. This type of stove burns naphtha, commonly called Coleman fuel or white gas, and is the hottest and most efficient kind of stove. All liquid fuel stoves work on the same principles. The gas is stored inside a fuel bottle or tank that you manually pressurize with a pump. The pressurized fuel passes through a fuel line that pre-heats and vaporizes it, then through a jet and burner that disperse the flame.

Most of these stoves use an external fuel bottle made of lightweight metal with a threaded opening that fits the stove pump and holds a lid when not in use. The fuel bottles come in different sizes so you can bring one or more that are just the right size

I have been using an MSR® WhisperLite Internationale™ Stove with a plastic pump for eight years and have never had a problem.

Be careful not to spill liquid stove fuel on your skin. Fuel has a very low freezing point and also evaporates very quickly, so it can cause frostbite in below-freezing temperatures. If you need to transfer fuel between containers, make a bottle holder in the snow and use a funnel.

for your trip. Some fuel bottles will have different sized threaded openings and will only accept pumps made by their company to be used with their bottles.

Some manufacturers make their pumps out of plastic and others out of metal. Plastic is generally lighter but can get melted or broken if neglected. Metal pumps are more and durable but weigh and cost more. Both work very well.

Most of these stoves need to be primed before lighting by filling a priming cup below the burner with liquid fuel, then burning off this fuel to heat up the fuel line. This allows the liquid fuel to vaporize in the fuel line and come out as a gas. It is this priming process, combined with the manual pumping, that makes liquid fuel stoves seem trickier to use than other types, but they're really not difficult once you understand how they work. Read the instruction manual to learn the specific operating procedures for your stove.

Multi-Fuel Stoves

Multi-fuel stoves are liquid fuel stoves with modifications to the fuel jet and burner to allow them to burn a variety of other fuels besides white gas, such as kerosene, diesel, aviation fuel or gasoline. These fuels are less refined and tend not to burn as well as white gas, so you will probably end up burning white gas in your stove unless you're traveling in a country where white gas is not available. Consider a multi-fuel stove if you think you may use it outside of the United States and Canada.

Liquefied Petroleum Gas (LPG) or Canister Stoves

LPG stoves, also known as canister stoves, have a small burner assembly that screws onto a sealed, pressurized LPG canister. LPG stoves are very lightweight and easy to use, but they produce less heat than liquid fuel stoves and are not a good choice for cold weather camping. The cold reduces the gas pressure in the canister and since there is no way to manually pressurize the canister, the heat output suffers, to the point that you might not even be able to boil water most of the time. Also, LPG canisters are bulky when you have to carry a lot of them for a longer trip. They are non-refillable and you will have to pack the empty ones out and find someplace that will recycle them.

If you have to use a canister stove, there are a few things you can do to improve the efficiency, but for your own confidence and safety, I highly recommend bringing a liquid fuel or multi-fuel stove instead. Keep the canister warm by keeping it in your jacket or sleeping bag for an hour or two before cooking. If you have any spare pieces of closed-cell foam, use some tape to make a foam sleeve to slip over your canister like a beer cozy to keep it warm when you aren't using it. Keep the canister off the snow by putting it on something like a piece of closed-cell foam or a cutting board. You can use a windscreen, but be very careful not to trap too much heat around the canister because this can create a fire or explosion hazard.

Cold reduces the gas pressure in canister stoves making them inefficient and potentially useless for winter camping. If you must use this type of stove try to keep the canister warm with body heat to increase the pressure.

Methyl Alcohol Stoves

Methyl alcohol stoves are very simple stoves that burn methyl alcohol. (They are so simple, in fact, that a rudimentary version can be made at home with an aluminum can and some solder.) These stoves are completely silent and have no moving parts, but they put out less heat than other types of stoves because the fuel is not pressurized. Alcohol does not burn well in cold weather, so these stoves are not recommended for winter use.

Burn Time and Fuel Consumption

Stoves vary in fuel efficiency and the manufacturer's specifications will tell you about the energy output of the stove, boiling rates and burn times for a given amount of fuel. Keep in mind that such ratings are similar to sleeping bag temperature ratings in that they are based on ideal conditions and will change significantly if you are melting snow for water and purifying water by boiling. But as a rule of thumb, you can be safe to use the following recommendations from MSR: about 6 fluid ounces (177 ml) of white gas per person per day when using the stove to melt snow/ice and boil water. In extremely cold temperatures, this increases to as much as 15 fluid ounces (445 ml).

Most manufacturers either include or sell separately a handy little repair/maintenance kit that comes with compact tools, common replacement parts and repair instructions.

Maximize the efficiency of your stove by putting a heat reflector underneath it and a windscreen around the outside of the burner and pot. The windscreen keeps the wind out and traps heat below the pot. It also acts as a heat shield between the burner and your fuel bottle. Stoves with a fuel bottle or canister attached directly below the burner are not recommended because they can overheat when used with a windscreen.

On an average two-night, three-day cold winter campout I usually burn 22 to 27 fluid ounces (650 to 800 ml). This will usually allow me to boil 8 to 9 quarts (8 to 9 L) of water from snow and cook pasta twice. It's not a bad idea to bring an extra bottle of fuel with you until you've learned exactly how much you use. Keep track of the temperature, how much cooking and water boiling you do and the amount of fuel you burn. Even once you are aware of how much you use, it's still a great idea to have an extra bottle in case of emergency.

Cooking in Your Vestibule

Never light your stove or cook inside your tent. Nylon is highly flammable and you don't want to risk burning down your tent—even if you escape unharmed you will have lost your shelter. Burning stoves can also use up all the oxygen in a tent and result in carbon monoxide poisoning. If you need to use your stove out of the elements, cook inside your tent vestibule, making sure that you clear away any clothing or gear and open the ventilation flap or door for air circulation. If you run into a problem, cover your stove with snow to extinguish the flames.

Stove Repair and Maintenance

You will need to clean your stove periodically and you might need to replace a few pieces here and there. You should always carry a repair kit for your stove.

Problems with liquid fuel stoves usually arise from residue clogging the jet, which is the pin-sized hole at the base of the burner that sprays fuel up to the burner. Some stoves have something called a shaker jet, which contains a needle that cleans out the hole when you shake the stove. Other stoves come with a special tool to clean the jet. You can help keep your jet clean by always burning clean fuel and always blowing out your flames when you turn off your stove. If you let the flames slowly burn out, they can leave behind a carbon residue that will build up, eventually leading to a clogged jet.

Vestibule cooking is sweet satisfaction when you are able to savor a cup of coffee without leaving the comfort of your sleeping bag.

BACKPACKS, PACKING & EQUIPMENT

Whether you're packing for a planned camping trip, or bringing camp gear on a long day trip as a safety precaution, you need to have something comfortable to carry everything in.

This chapter focuses on your next essential piece of winter backpacking equipment: the backpack. You'll learn how to choose and properly fit a backpack that is right for you, how to load your gear into a backpack in the most efficient way possible, and how to choose what to pack so you don't bring too much.

Backpacks: A New Piece of Anatomy

There are lots of ways to carry and protect your equipment when traveling in the winter. But 90% of the time, your tool of choice will be a backpack. This piece of gear is something you're probably already familiar with. You've probably toted one around at some point in your life. You may even have one sitting in your closet. But you'll want to pay special attention to choosing a backpack for use in the winter months.

Backpacks come in all different shapes and sizes, colors, brand names and materials. Don't go and buy one just because it looks cool or matches your outer shell layers. Follow the steps outlined below. Start by familiarizing yourself with the features available.

Chapter 3

Backpacks: A New Piece of Anatomy

How to Pack a Backpack

Packing Options and Technique

Sleds or Pulks: An Alternative to Backpacks

1. Lids *cover the top of the pack like a baseball cap and include a big pocket. This pocket can be used to store items that you need to access easily, such as a camera or a snack. The lid may also be extendible and/or floating. An extendible lid is one that can totally detach from the main portion of the backpack (some can even serve as a hip belt or fanny pack for day trips). A floating lid allows you to loosen the straps that attach the lid to the main portion of the pack so you can overstuff the main compartment or stow a sleeping pad or a jacket under the lid. Extendible and floating lids are great features.*

2. Stabilizer straps *are found where the shoulder straps and the waist/hip belts meet the body of the backpack. When tightened, they cinch the bag closer to the body for a snug but comfortable fit, which also helps transfer the weight of the pack to your legs.*

3. Sternum straps *have a buckle that clips both of your shoulder straps together in front of your chest. This feature allows for a better fit and makes the backpack feel more secure on your back.*

Then narrow down your choice by looking for packs that have the amount of volume that you need and the specific features you want. The final step is to ensure a proper, comfortable fit. Fit is the key to a good backpack and an enjoyable experience.

Your ultimate goal is to have a backpack that fits so comfortably that you think of it as part of your anatomy. Choose wisely and this amazing piece of gear will be a buddy of yours forever, following you on every epic journey around the world!

Backpack Terminology and Features

• **Volume** refers to the amount of space or room inside the whole backpack. Volume is measured in cubic inches or liters.

• **Back length** refers to the different sizes available to fit different people's backs. Some also have harnesses that can be adjusted to change the distance between the shoulder straps and the hip belt.

• **Top-loading** packs are designed to be packed through a large hole in the top. In my opinion, this is the best design. If you pack a top-loader correctly, anything that you need during the day will be accessible at the top and you won't have to worry about pockets with zippers that may wear out and break in the field.

It makes sense that the stronger, heavier people in your group will carry the heavier gear, like pots and pans, or shared shelter equipment. Your goal should be to carry no more than 25% of your weight, and ideally closer to 10-15% for maximum comfort and enjoyment.

4. Waist/hip belts *are best when designed for load-bearing. A load-bearing hip belt is a padded belt at the bottom of the backpack that clips together around your hips. When properly adjusted, it transfers all of the pack's weight directly to your hips and legs. Without this feature, your shoulders would bear all the weight, resulting in major discomfort and fatigue.*

5. Compression straps *are found on the sides of a backpack. They are used to tighten up the pack as a final adjustment. This helps to secure the load and minimize the size of your backpack.*

It's best to avoid extra zippers on your gear (especially backpacks) when possible because they are just one more thing that can break in the field. If a zipper blows on any of your gear, the first thing you should try is squeezing the zipper slider using a pair of pliers on your multi-tool to create more tension. This will often be enough to keep your zipper from splitting again for a while. Most zippers today are made of a plastic coil instead of metal or plastic teeth. Often enough you can zip over the split and back (with a bit of force) and it will fix itself as long as the slider is tight enough.

• *Panel-loading* packs are divided into as many as six different compartments and pockets. There may be a bottom compartment, a main compartment, a lid with a pocket, and pockets on both sides and the front. People often like the look of these packs and appreciate being able to organize gear into separate compartments.

Construction is important to consider when comparing backpacks. Take a look on the inside of the backpack, as well as at all of the seams and buckles. The seams inside of the backpack should be taped (covered with another piece of material). Taped, sealed seams will minimize the amount of water or moisture that can seep into the pack and prevent the seams from wearing prematurely. Make sure that the inside of the pack has a rubbery, polyurethane coating for water resistance. Also make sure any zippers look beefy and durable. I often suggest avoiding having any zippers on your pack if possible, aside from the zipper on the lid pocket, because they are just one more thing that can break in the field.

Materials are also important to consider. The material your pack is made of will affect its weight, durability, price, and water-resistance. The two most common materials are pack cloth and cordura. Pack cloth is a lightweight nylon material that sheds water very well. Cordura is much more abrasion-resistant and durable—and usually more affordable—but is heavier and absorbs more water than pack cloth. Some backpacks use both materials in combination to create a strong, affordable and fairly light backpack.

Thermo-molded padding is a feature I'd place in the "bells and whistles" category. Thermo-molding is a process in which the closed-cell foam used to make your hip belt, shoulder straps and back is heated and molded into an anatomical shape. This process increases comfort and ensures that there will be no deformation in the straps as the backpack wears.

Categories of Backpacks

Now that you're familiar with some of the features to look for in a backpack, consider what size of pack you'll need. Backpacks are generally categorized by volume.

Day Packs: 2,000 cu. in. (35 L) or less

Day packs have just enough volume to pack all that you need for a day out on the trail (water bottle, light shell jacket, snacks, first aid kit, knife, radio). Day packs usually have a waist stabilizer instead of a load-bearing hip belt.

Weekend/Overnight: 2,000–3,350 cu. in. (35–55 L)

These mid-sized packs, also called alpine packs, have enough room for one or two nights out. They usually have a padded, load-bearing hip belt and a floating lid. Some have compression straps so you can cinch down the bag to a smaller size if you don't need all the space, a great feature that lets you use it as a day pack as well.

Backpacking: 3,350–4,600 cu. in. (55–75 L)

This is a really good size for extended overnight trips. These large packs should have a load-bearing hip belt, comfortable-fitting shoulder straps and a sternum strap.

If you do have a zipper that cannot be fixed, you can zip the slider ahead of the damaged area and sew the split portion together with a few loops of strong thread. If there will be substantial force on the zipper, like a backpack zipper, use fishing line because it will stretch a lot more than thread before breaking.

Multi-day/Expedition: 4,600–6,700 cu. in. (75–110 L)

These spacious packs are intended for extreme use in the outdoors on extended multi-day trips (two to four weeks). These packs are also ideal for winter trips as you require more fuel and gear than most other seasons of travel. Be careful when packing if you have a backpack of this size, however. The bigger the backpack, the more unnecessary stuff you'll be tempted to bring—so just remember that you'll be the one carrying it all!

Sizing and Fitting a Backpack

After finding a pack with the volume and features you need, it's time to put it to the real test. Your backpack needs to fit properly and be comfortable to wear. A backpack should direct almost all of the weight to your hips, letting your legs (not your shoulders and back) do all of the work. To do this, it must conform closely to the shape of your body with minimal restriction, and not feel cumbersome or cause any pressure points.

The biggest mistake you can make is choosing a pack that has a torso too long or too short for your back. This will throw off all the other adjustments you make to the pack. Remember that tall people can have short torsos and shorter people can have longer torsos, so really focus on your own body type and what fits you best.

Before you walk out of the store with your top-of-the-line pack, you should make sure that you've got the right size and fit, ideally with the assistance of a knowledgeable staff member in the store. The following guidelines will not only help you find the right bag for you; they are also useful steps to follow every time you load up your pack when you're ready to hit the trails.

1. Have someone at the store load the pack with around 30 to 40 pounds. You won't be able to tell if a pack is right for you without loading the bag with weight, adjusting it properly, and wearing it for a while.

2. Loosen off all of the straps—shoulders, hip, sternum, compression straps and lid. Now put this sloppy and heavy pack on your back. Have the store staff give you a hand if required.

3. Bend way over as if to touch your toes, then flop the pack up high on your back, clip together the hip belt and tighten it snug as possible around the top of your waist. Now stand up and let the pack slide down on your body. The hip belt should be resting securely around your waist, the big hip buckle should be centered with your

bellybutton, and your hip bones should be in the center of the hip belt pads.

4. Now grab the shoulder harness straps and tighten them both evenly. This will bring the pack closer to your back, creating a more inline balance with your body. The pack should feel lighter now that your hips and legs are taking most of the load. The pack should feel snug and balanced, not pulling to either side. If it's not balanced, loosen and readjust the shoulder straps, making sure that both are equalized. Don't over-tighten; this will cause a big crease in the straps at the top of your shoulders. The shoulder straps should curve smoothly around your shoulders to your back with minimal space between the padding and your body.

5. Clip the sternum strap and tighten.

6. Now begin to evenly tighten the stabilizer straps at the top of the pack and the ones that can sometimes be found running from the hip belt to the body of the backpack. They should slope down from the pack to the shoulders at a 45-degree angle. Don't over-tighten, which can result in major discomfort and a nasty tension headache. Cinch up the compression straps. Your pack should feel comfortable and balanced, and put next to no weight on your shoulders. Remember you are looking for a fit that really conforms to the natural shape of your body. If you don't get it from the first pack, try on other packs until you find the right one.

Pack your fuel below your food so it won't spoil your food if it leaks. Of course, you can also prevent leaks by ensuring that lids are properly sealed before packing!

Special Notes about Fitting Backpacks for Women

Women generally have shorter torsos, narrower shoulders, and bigger hips and chests than men. So it's no surprise that it can be difficult to get a perfect fit out of a backpack designed for a man. A backpack designed for women will have shoulder straps that are closer together and straps that are a little narrower and shorter. The hip belts are tapered and come in different lengths to conform better to a woman's hips.

It's now easier than ever for women to shop for outdoor gear that will fit properly, because many companies now offer clothing and gear such as backpacks and sleeping bags tailored specifically to fit women's bodies.

How to Pack a Backpack

Packing a backpack properly can make a huge difference to your balance, comfort and safety. It's also important to do well to ensure the protection and accessibility of your gear. It will take you a bit of time to perfect a packing system that works for you and uses the space efficiently, but here are some essentials to help you get started. To put it simply, good packing accomplishes two things: easy access to the things you need, and balanced weight distribution.

Four rules when packing a backpack.

1. Imagine that filling up your pack with gear is like pouring cement into a hole. There

1. Mid/Light *The lid compartment is the space you'll use the most during the day, and should contain all the items you'll need easy access to while on the move—items like your multi-tool or knife, matches, map, lunch or snacks, extra hat, and headlamp.*

2. Light *The very top of your pack should also be fairly light. If your pack is top-heavy, you'll be pulled off balance and waste energy trying to stay upright. The top of your pack is a good place to put things you might want during the day that are too big to fit in the lid pocket, like a down jacket or any layers that you strip off as you travel. Try not to overstuff your pack to the point where the top is way above your head!*

3. Light *The section of the pack that is farthest away from your body's center of gravity should be as light as possible. Otherwise, you'll feel like you're being pulled backwards. Once you've packed areas 1, 2 and 3, fill area 4 with your tent, or whatever part of a shared tent you're carrying. To minimize bulk and spread the weight over a wide area, remove the fly and body of the tent from its stuff sack and stuff each one separately into all the hard-to-fill nooks and crannies (think "pouring cement").*

4. Medium *Fill this section with spare clothing, lighter equipment and food.*

5. Heavy *Keep your heaviest gear—pots, stove, tent poles, heavy food, fuel and any extra water that you won't need access to during the day—close to your back and down low so it's in line with your spine and directly above your hips and legs. Try to pack it in a way so that nothing will be sticking out and digging into your back.*

6. Light *The space in the pack below the top of your butt should be filled with relatively light gear. If the weight is too heavy here, it can push in on your lower back and make it uncomfortable and harder to hike. A ground sheet or tarp goes perfectly here, adding a barrier between the wet ground and any gear packed above it. Next, pack your sleeping bag because it's light and won't need to be unpacked until the end of the day.*

should be no empty gaps or pockets when you're done. Empty spaces just waste space and can lead to an awkwardly shaped and imbalanced pack.

2. Fill your bag with items in order of daily use. Don't pack your rain jacket and lunch at the bottom and your sleeping bag and stove on top. Everything you might need during the day should be stored in the top lid pocket so that you never have to open your pack during the day. At most you should only have to unbuckle the lid to reach an extra layer or a rain jacket stored underneath. You should only have to dig into the body of your pack once you're in camp.

3. There should be no dangling gear attached to the outside of your pack. If there is, it means that you have either over-packed or have not packed efficiently enough. Dangling gear can get damaged, fall off, or simply clang around and drive you and your hiking partners crazy. Besides, it's just not cool!

Even if packed correctly your bag may be rather heavy. To avoid strain injuries when putting on your backpack set it on a rock or ledge and back into the straps or have someone support the weight until your arms are in the straps.

Nest things together or store stuff inside each other. Nesting your stove, matches, fuel pump, scrubby and stove repair kit inside of your pot set is a great way to save space and keep gear that you need together, together!

Even in the coldest and driest weather, snow can build up on your pack or sled and melt. For this reason it's always a good idea to waterproof everything that you need to keep dry.

4. The weight of your pack should be balanced evenly and follow the weight distribution pattern described on page 57, from bottom to top.

Take your time placing your equipment inside your pack and try to visualize how everything can fit together like a puzzle, keeping the weight distribution in mind. When you're done, you can take pride in your backpack as a piece of art that's well-organized, symmetrical and well balanced!

Waterproofing Your Gear

Picture this. It's bright and sunny, early on your departure day. You're all ready for your long-anticipated winter camping trip. The weather is perfect, not a cloud for a thousand miles. But you must waterproof your gear!

Too often I've seen someone wind up very unhappy and uncomfortable at the end of a day because they didn't follow this rule. The weather can change, you might drop your pack or slip into a stream. A water bottle that wasn't closed tightly enough leaks inside your pack.

In winter temperatures, any of these things can result in a very serious situation. Your backpack might have a rubbery polyurethane inner coating and taped seams to make it water-resistant, but this does not make it waterproof. Many seams will still leak, and anywhere there's a zipper or a drawstring, water will be able to come through.

It can take hours of effort and attention to dry out something like a wet sleeping bag in the field, but it only takes a few extra minutes to waterproof everything before you even leave on your trip. It's worth it to know that no matter what happens during the day, you will have a warm, dry haven to retreat to—your dry shelter, your dry sleeping bag and your dry clothes.

There are a few different ways to waterproof your gear. You can start by purchasing a rain cover for your pack—a piece of rubber-coated nylon with big elastic band sewn around the outside rim. Some packs come with a rain cover already, tucked into a small pocket just behind the lid. A rain cover alone will not guarantee to keep your gear dry, but it is one part of a good waterproofing system with some redundancies built in.

Another option is to use dry bags. Designed primarily for kayaking and canoeing, dry bags are durable, rubber-coated nylon or vinyl bags that come in a variety of different sizes measured in cubic inches or liters. They have a roll-top closure with a buckle that seals the bag once you've packed it and squeezed all the air out. They are durable and waterproof when sealed correctly. Look for them in paddlesport shops or in the paddling section of an outdoor store. Rubber-coated nylon bags are more expensive but they slide more easily into and out of your pack; vinyl bags are less expensive and very durable but they tend to stick to each other.

Rain jackets and backpack rain covers should be kept in the most accessible compartments in the event of a quick change in weather.

If you already have some dry bags or the concept appeals to you, you can definitely make it work. However, because dry bags, particularly the vinyl ones, can be a bit bulky and awkward to pack into a backpack, you can also just save a bit of money and use garbage bags instead.

Waterproofing a Sleeping Bag with a Garbage Bag

Here's how to do it properly:

1. Line your sleeping bag stuff sack with a garbage bag and roll the excess garbage bag out over the top of the stuff sack as if you were lining a garbage bin.

2. Stuff your sleeping bag foot-first into the garbage bag inside the stuff sack. (If you stuff the sleeping bag headfirst, air will be trapped inside the sleeping bag and it will be a lot harder to stuff.)

3. Once the sleeping bag is stuffed in the bag, pull up the excess garbage bag and bunch it loosely in your hand, leaving a finger-sized opening for air to escape. Use your hands and chest to squish all of the air out of the bag. I call this "pruning."

4. Once you have gotten as much air as possible out of the bag, twist the excess garbage bag like a pigtail so that no air can get back in.

Left: You can get dry bags in a variety of sizes for different purposes: for example, a medium-sized one for your sleeping bag, smaller ones to use exclusively for food and a larger one for your clothes. Right: Make sure the garbage bag does not slip in when you are packing the bag because fishing it out 'post-packing' can sometimes lead to rips.

Never roll up a sleeping bag and put it in a stuff sack—especially if it has synthetic insulation. Synthetic insulation has "memory". Every time you fold and flatten it, it loses some of its loft. Stuffing your bag extends its life by ensuring that it takes on a different shape every time you pack it up.

Always pack extra bags: grocery, garbage and small sealable ones (like Ziploc). You never know when you might need them! Sealable bags come in handy for packing out trash or for storing leftover meals. They're also great for waterproofing your book or journal.

5. You can put an elastic around the pigtail to make sure it stays closed, but if you've twisted it tight enough it will stay closed on its own. Tuck the pigtail into the stuff sack and pull the drawstring closed. Now your sleeping bag is 100% waterproof and the garbage bag is protected against tears by the stuff sack!

You can use this same process for packing clothes. You might want to fold your dry clothes before putting them into a stuff sack. I find that the square, flat shape of folded clothes is easier to pack, as well as easier to pack things around.

A set of complete packing lists are included in the appendix.

Packing Options and Technique

Most of us have a tendency to pack more than we need. Often, the bigger the backpack, the more stuff we bring. This unnecessary weight is a real drag, especially in the winter when you already have more and bulkier gear. You need to be extra careful to bring only what you need.

Deciding What to Bring

The following are some suggestions for packing for a winter trip. I still follow this process on every single trip I head out on. I like to think I have a really good system, but this process always helps me to be even more selective and efficient.

Start off by making a list of every single thing that you think you will need. I recommend that you use the lists included in the appendix as your main guidelines and personalize them as required. Don't leave anything out.

Pack all your different categories of gear and equipment in different-colored stuff sacks. This will make it easier to find what you're looking for and it helps to keep things organized.

You can even draw a chess/checkerboard on your closed cell foam pad with permanent marker for some evening entertainment.

Next, clear off your bed or living room floor and take every item on your list and lay it out so that you can see it. Group your gear into different sections: sleeping and shelter; cooking and food; active clothes; dry clothes; entertainment (music player, book, journal); and miscellaneous (headlamp, repair kit and first aid kit).

Now that everything is all laid out in front of you, start removing all the things you know you don't really need or will not likely use and put them in a pile off to the side. For example, you don't really need a multi-tool, Swiss Army knife, and a single-blade knife; just pack the multi-tool. Don't bring a cup and a mug; just bring the mug. Instead of a bowl and a plate, just bring the bowl—better yet, choose a large mug and then use it as both a mug and a bowl! Now take a look at the stuff you've removed. You will be amazed at how much you've eliminated, reducing weight, bulk and the stress of trying to fit it into your backpack.

For the Ultra Hard Core

If you want to be ultra hard core, you're still not finished. Reduce any duplications of purpose. For example, if you are thinking of bringing a closed-cell foam pad and Therm-a-Rest for extra comfort and warmth, just bring the most important one, the closed-cell foam. Then take a good look at all the remaining gear and make sure you don't pack anything that doesn't serve at least two purposes. For example, your closed-cell sleeping pad can also serve as a splint for first aid, your stove's windscreen can be used as a funnel, and dental floss can be used for emergency sewing repairs. This process can help you send more gear to the discard pile. You can further reduce the weight of your pack by fractions of ounces by sawing the handle off your toothbrush, chopping the margins off the pages of your book, opting to make all your utensils out of twigs and sticks in the field, and removing the cardboard centers of your toilet paper rolls. Use your imagination and think of how you can use single items for multiple purposes!

Although you want to bring the least possible amount of gear, be careful not to cut back to the point that you don't have enough to be comfortable and safe. After all, you want to have fun on your winter trip! Make sure to treat yourself and pack one luxury item you don't want to leave without, like a pair of silk long underwear to sleep in, or some really fine chocolate.

Packing Clothing

When packing clothing, divide everything into the two categories that I discussed back in Chapter 1: active clothes and dry clothes. First, set aside all the layers that you will be wearing when you leave to head out into the field in the morning. These are your active clothes. You will remove and add these layers continually throughout the day to regulate your heat and moisture, every day that you are out.

The rest of your clothes are your dry clothes and should be waterproofed and packed in

You might want to leave a complete set of clean, dry street clothes in your vehicle at the trailhead that you can look forward to changing into at the end of a winter campout. This luxury will make the ride home a lot more comfortable and will minimize the sniff-'n'-stare that you might get in the coffee shop pit-stop on the way home. I also like to leave a favorite snack in the car, one that I just can't wait to pig out on—great motivation for the last leg of a trip.

your backpack, to be pulled out only when you are in camp at the very end of the day, or in your tent or shelter.

The only exception is your down jacket, which you may want to quickly pull on anytime that you're not moving. I keep mine tucked under the lid of my backpack so that when I stop for a break, I can put it on before my body cools down too much. When it's time to move again, the jacket is easy to tuck away. Like your other dry clothes, it should be waterproofed anytime you're not wearing it.

Before You Pack Anything

Before departing on your trip, check to make sure all pieces of equipment are in good working order and that nothing needs any repairs. Here's a little checklist:

• *Fire up your stove* and let it burn for a few minutes to make sure it works properly. Replace and fix anything you think you might have a problem with in the field.

• *Check that your tent* has all its pieces including the fly. Make sure that there are no broken or missing poles and that there are no holes in the body of the tent or the fly.

Things can get uncomfortable and even dangerous very quickly in the field if you discover that major components of your gear are not working or are missing. Remember, PREVENTION, PREVENTION, PREVENTION. Most accidents or mishaps can be prevented simply by taking the time to prepare for your trip properly.

Sleds or Pulks: An Alternative to Backpacks

Another way to transport your gear on a winter trip is using a sled, also called a pulk, loaded with all your gear waterproofed in smaller packs and duffel bags. Your gear and equipment are packed inside the sled and secured to it. The sled is then attached to a smaller alpine pack on your back or attached to your waist with a harness. This method of travel is typically used on longer expeditions where you have more food, fuel and equipment than you could ever carry comfortably on your back. There are advantages and disadvantages to this method. It's up to you to decide which are most important to you, depending on your personal ideals and trip objectives.

ADVANTAGES

• great for longer trips
• can store up to a month's worth of equipment
• typically used in open terrain such as mountain glaciers, open lakes and Arctic or Antarctic polar trips
• easier to pack and unpack than a backpack
• fun to slide down hills on!
• easy and fun to make your own customized sled

Food=energy and energy=ability to survive the cold so you want to double check your stove and fuel situations carefully.

- can be difficult to use in mixed or heavy forested terrain
- can be frustrating on steeper terrain
- can be expensive to purchase a new sled
- may cause lower back discomfort at first

I really like using a sled on winter trips, especially trips lasting three or more days. I have built a few of my own for around $30 each and they have been used and abused but they keep on trucking. Although sled-hauling in heavy forest and steep hills can be a challenge at times, you can definitely master the art of bushwhacking with a sled. I can now bunny-hop mine over logs and two-and-a-half-foot fences without skipping a beat, but it takes practice.

There are many 'recipes' for sled making online. Just be sure to choose one that has crossed spacer bars as they make a world of difference when turning.

Avoiding hang-ups when bushwhacking is a skill that comes with practice.

WINTER TRAVEL

Now that you've got all your gear packed up and ready to go, you're going to have to get around with it. In this chapter, I'll cover the many common ways you can travel in winter. I'll start with the simplest self-propelled methods and progress into those that are bit more involved and equipment-dependent.

Chapter 4

Hiking in Your Boots

Snowshoeing

Cross-Country Skiing

Getting Around in the Mountains

Skijoring

Dog Sledding

Hiking in Your Boots

A warm, simple way to go is to hike in snow boots, or to use waterproofed leather hikers with a pair of gaiters to keep the snow out. Snow boots mean those knee-high, waterproof winter boots with the removable felt liners.

When the snow isn't very deep, hiking in good boots can be the easiest way to travel, but if the snow is deeper, you'll sink in and it will make for slow going, and be very tiring.

When you're trying to decide whether hiking in boots is an appropriate choice for your trip, be sure to check the weather forecast—what are the chances that the snow will remain as shallow as it was when you set out? For safety's sake, you must factor in how long it will take to travel if the conditions change dramatically.

Hiking boots work great as long as you don't have deep snow to deal with.

Some outfitters offer snowshoe rentals so you can try out a few different styles before committing to a purchase. If you do take snowshoes for a test drive, try them out on some different types of terrain to see how they perform.

Snowshoeing

Snowshoeing originated roughly 6,000 years ago in Central Asia. According to some theories, snowshoes made it possible for people from Asia to cross over the Bering Land Bridge to North America. Whether you're crossing continents or just going for a short trek, snowshoeing is a great way to get around on snow because it keeps you from sinking in—and if you know how to walk, it's easy to learn how to do it!

More refined technique will come with time and miles put on your snowshoes but the following should help you to get started. Once you have borrowed or purchased your own pair of snowshoes, spend an afternoon or two in the field with them before you try them out with a fully loaded backpack. I also recommend that you do some practice hikes with a loaded backpack before heading out on an overnighter. This will give you a bit of time to get used to using your snowshoes with weight on your back, and set you up for success when you head out for the real thing.

Snowshoe Terminology

Here are some common snowshoe parts and terms that you should know when looking for a pair of snowshoes:

Flotation describes the snowshoe's buoyancy in the snow. The more surface area a shoe has, the less you will sink in soft snow. The type of decking also affects the amount of flotation. Modern decking, usually made of a synthetic material with no holes in it, such as Hypalon, provides more flotation than the old-school tennis racket–style woven snowshoes.

1. Decking *is the term for the material that creates the barrier between the top of the shoe and the snow. Decking provides flotation on the snow, as well as a place to attach the harness, binding and crampon.*

2. Heel lifts *or steppers are typically found on mountaineering snowshoes. A heel lift is a piece of hard plastic that flips up underneath your heel to add an inch or so of space between your boot and the snowshoe. The main purpose is to reduce foot and calf muscle fatigue when climbing steep or very long hills.*

3. Bindings *attach the harness to the main part of the snowshoe, allowing your foot to pivot each time you lift your leg to take a step. Two basic systems exist: elastic band and bar plate pivot.*

4. Crampons *are the sharp metallic spikes located on the bottom of the snowshoe below the ball of your foot and the heel that aid in traction on icy and technical terrain.*

5. Harnesses *connect your boots to your snowshoes. There are many different designs and styles. Which one you choose depends on your budget, the terrain you usually travel in, and personal preference.*

Three Basic Styles of Snowshoes

There are three basic styles of snowshoes. Here's how to spot them, as well as a brief overview of their advantages and disadvantages.

Beavertail, Michigan or Maine

Shaped like a beaver's tail, these snowshoes have a wide, rounded front with a turned-up nose, tapering at the back like a teardrop with a very narrow tail.

Advantages: Great all-around shape for trails, open woods and fields.

Disadvantages: Awkward in super-deep, powdery snow or heavy bush.

Alaskan, Yukon or Trail

These snowshoes are very long and narrower than the beavertail, with a big, upturned nose and a tapered tail.

Advantages: Great for really deep snow and long distances in big, open areas.

Disadvantages: Poor maneuverability; not so good in the bush

Bear Paw

These snowshoes have an oval shape that is almost round, a turned-up nose, and no tail.

Advantages: Great maneuverability in thick bush and hilly areas.

Disadvantages: Lack of a tail means they don't track as straight; large surface area accumulates snow on top of the shoe, reducing performance in deep snow.

Traditional-Style Snowshoes – Materials and Construction

Many traditional designs are based on the naturally efficient shapes of animal paws and are still used today. For example, today's very long Yukon or Alaskan-style snowshoe, which works well in very deep snow and is great for long-distance travel, is based on ancient models that were over 7 feet long.

Frames on traditional snowshoes are typically made from ash, a type of wood which is very strong and can stand up to a lot of use. Traditional decking is made from sinew (animal guts); and bindings from leather. These materials will last for many years if you care for your snowshoes diligently. Leather bindings need to be kept moist and supple with a bit of mink oil or similar treatment applied once or twice a season. It also helps to add a new coat of shellac to the sinew and lacing. Every couple of seasons, you can add a new coat of varnish to the wooden frame to keep the wood sealed and to prevent any rotting or cracking.

Most traditional designs have a turned-up nose to prevent the shoes from scooping up snow with every step. The long, skinny tails help the shoe to track while you're hiking. The woven sinew decking, which looks a bit like a tennis racket, offers some traction.

Modern Snowshoes – Materials and Construction

Most modern snowshoes are made from an alloy, typically aluminum, which is very lightweight and strong. The most common shape is a rounded rectangle with a turned-up nose. Most have crampons and heel lifts or steppers. They are fairly light, very durable and require almost no maintenance. There are quite a few considerations when selecting a modern snowshoe—shape, construction, features and cost. Prices for a decent beginner set start at around $100.

Different decking materials such as plastic and Hypalon vary in stiffness and durability. Do some research and choose something that will stand up in the terrain you will be traveling over most of the time. I find that softer decks are more fatiguing, especially on softer, deeper snow.

There are many different foot harness systems such as straps, buckles and ratchets. Again, this largely comes down to personal preference. You might find you like the ease and simplicity of cinching straps. Some people find buckles are too hard to adjust with mitts on, while others find that ratcheting buckles, while likely to snag in heavy brush, are perfect for use with mountaineering boots.

Modern snowshoes use either an elastic band or a pivot bar system for bindings. The elastic band system works really well in thickly wooded areas where you need to step over and around things, because it keeps some tension on the shoe so that the tail doesn't drop straight to the ground every time you take a step. The downside is that the shoe may not shed snow as easily as a bar plate system and in certain snow conditions can become heavy.

The bar plate system sheds snow very well and is also great for steep hills and more technical terrain. The free-pivoting binding allows you to use your crampons more aggressively—you can even climb a ladder with this design. In thick woods, however, the loose tails of your snowshoes are more likely to get hung up.

Getting the Right Size and Fit

To determine the proper snowshoe size, consider these two things: your total body

Traditional snowshoes are better suited for walking on flat open areas as they are larger and do not have crampons that are much-needed for climbing steep terrain.

weight (including the heaviest pack weight you will ever plan to carry) and the type of terrain and snow conditions you will generally travel on. Generally, you will need one square inch of surface area per pound of weight on your snowshoes.

Here's a great way to develop a new appreciation for snowshoes. First, find a clear area with some deep snow, establish start and finish lines, and race each other with snowshoes on. Congratulate the winner. Then remove your snowshoes and repeat the same race.

Modern snowshoes allow you to walk more naturally because they are much narrower than the traditional ones that force you to straddle.

Manufacturers will often have their own specific scale and sizing, but here are some common sizing options. The first measurement is the width of the snowshoe and the second is the length of the snowshoe.

8" x 25" = 100 to 175 lbs

9" x 30" = 175 to 250 lbs

10" x 36" = 250 lbs +

Children's shoes are rated for 100 pounds or less.

What Kind of Footwear Should I Use?

My favorite snowshoeing boots are mid-height leather hiking boots with a full gusseted tongue. This style of boot usually fits great with any type of harness and binding system and they are also nice for hiking. Just make sure you waterproof and lace them as described in the Chapter 1 section on footwear to keep your feet warm. Gaiters are essential for this type of boot as the snow will be deeper than the top of your boots and it is critical that you keep your feet as dry as possible.

Snow boots can work as well. Just make sure that you try your snowshoes on with your intended footwear for, to make sure that your boots fit properly inside the snowshoe harness system while allowing proper blood circulation to your toes.

Whatever boots you use with your snowshoes, make sure they are waterproofed.

Snowshoe Technique

The basic athletic stance is relatively the same in all sports: hockey, volleyball, basketball and snowboarding. Standing with your legs spread slightly apart, knees slightly bent, and arms just out from your sides lowers your center of gravity, improves your balance and stacks your body weight vertically for more stability. The same applies for snowshoeing, especially if you are wearing a loaded backpack. Use of this basic body position will mostly come into play on your ascents, descents and in rougher terrain.

Getting Around on Flats

If your backpack is properly loaded and the weight distribution is even, you should find it fairly easy to move along. If there is a hard crust of snow on top that you keep breaking through, you might find that you need to slow down and take higher steps to keep the nose of your snowshoes from getting caught under the crust.

Climbing and Descending

Route planning and picking safe lines are a great skills to have for climbing or descending any hill. As the gradient and terrain change, you need to be looking ahead and planning where you want to go and where you don't want to go. Scan the hill to find the path of least resistance. Look for obstacles like icy sections, sticks and branches, logs and fallen trees that might be difficult to get over with a loaded backpack.

Your technique will differ from hill to hill and you will also have to adjust to the snow conditions. The three different snow conditions that you will most often have to contend with are: deep, dry powder; deep powder or corn snow with a thick layer of crust; and heavy, wet snow.

When climbing, maintain a balanced center of gravity by keeping your knees over your toes and your chest over your knees. You need to keep your weight over your feet. It's a similar principle to putting heavy blocks in the back of a vehicle to keep weight over the wheels.

When descending, make sure to keep your knees bent and your shoes flat to the terrain so that as much of the snowshoe as possible comes into contact with the snow, and so that your crampons (if you have them) will bite. Keep your arms out in front of you, or to your sides for extra balance and stabilization. If you lean too far forward, you might do a somersault, but it you lean too far back, you'll lose critical surface contact and start sliding. Keep your head up so you can constantly gauge the terrain ahead and react accordingly.

Depending on the snow conditions, you may want to try one or a combination of the following techniques.

Circulation of blood to your feet is vital in the prevention of frostbite. Once you have the right sized gear, make sure you do not tighten your boots or snowshoes in the field so much that you restrict blood flow to your feet and toes.

• **Use long traverses or switchbacks.** Instead of going straight down the fall line (the quickest line to the bottom), walk from top to bottom by crossing the slope of the hill on an angle, thereby cutting the steepness in half. You can link a series of these traverses together in a zigzag pattern to create a switchback.

• **Stomp your step** a couple of times before putting real weight on it. This will compact the snow into a more solid and stable depression for each step, giving you more balance and stability.

Left: Stack your weight on your snowshoe, digging your crampon in, and commit when ascending hills. Right: Switchbacks may seem like a waste of energy because it means taking the longer route. However, just as you get more tired sprinting 100 yards than walking 200, switchbacks are less demanding on you physically and will help you conserve your energy for the long haul.

• **Kick steps with your toes** when the terrain is very steep, or when there is a thick layer of crust on the snow. Take a couple of kicks into the front of the hill to create a solidly packed pocket for you to step on. To climb, when you step up onto one leg, make sure you shift your body weight directly above that foot. Repeat the same process with your opposite foot, kicking steps all the way up the hill. You can perform the same technique descending by walking backwards, kicking your toes into the slope of the hill for better traction and purchase. Descending backwards also allows you to use your hands for balance if the hill is steep enough.

• **Side step** by placing yourself sideways against a slope and stomp yourself a big staircase into the side of the hill. This is a great way to feel a little more balanced and creates more overall surface area for you to stand on. It also makes the climb or descent a lot easier for the all the people on your trip who are following you. Who knows, you might even get an extra serving of dessert for all your work!

• **Herringbone**, a technique used in cross-country skiing, is a way of climbing a hill straight-on with your toes pointed out and your heels close together to make a V-shape with your feet. This allows you to use the inside edges of your snowshoes and also creates a bit of a stair with every step.

• **Take off your snowshoes** if things are just not working out and you are getting frustrated. Even if your hiking boots sink deep into the snow, you'll get good grip and more control.

Overall, your snowshoe technique will become more natural and efficient with time and practice. You just need to spend some time on your shoes and put the miles in!

Left: Stomping your step while side stepping allows you more control with better purchase on the snow. Right: You may not look the coolest doing the herringbone step but it is far better than a face-plant when your snowshoe slips out from under you.

Cross-Country Skiing

When you put on cross-country skis—also known as Nordic skis—you're taking part in an activity with a long and illustrious history. Cross-country skis were originally developed in Northern Europe and Scandinavia over 4,000 years ago. There's mention of cross-country skiing in Viking histories. In Norway, medieval kings had to be good at it to prove that they were well-rounded athletes.

Cross-country skiing is a fun way to travel. Depending on the conditions, you'll sometimes be forced to more or less walk on your skis much the same way you would with snowshoes, but in other conditions, trading snowshoes for skis will make the difference between trudging through the snow or gliding over it!

In general, dogs are not welcome on most cross country trails because they ruin the tracks made by groomers or other skiers, so leave them at home unless you are breaking your own trail or are heading out in a dog-friendly area.

Second-hand stores often have plenty of overlooked skis that are perfectly fine for recreational use. Even old-fashioned wood ones still have a lot to offer as long as they are the right size for you.

Boots, Bindings and Poles

If you decide to go cross-country skiing for a winter camping trip, you'll need an extra set of skiing-specific boots that fit into your cross-country ski bindings, in addition to the winter boots that you might bring for walking around at camp once you take your skis off. While this extra pair of boots adds some weight to what you bring, it's great to have a pair available at the end of the day that you haven't been sweating into for a few hours.

There are all kinds of binding systems out there, from the more old-fashioned "three-pin" which clips the toe of the boot into the binding, to the modern New Nordic Norm (NNN) and Salomon Nordic System (SNS) bindings which not only clip the toe in, but also help guide the heel of the boot into the right spot with each stride. Boots can be waterproofed with grocery bags the same way as leather winter boots. Both types of boots are usually warm enough with a single pair of wool or synthetic socks, and you can keep snow out with your gaiters.

Poles for cross-country skiing should fit to about your armpit when you are standing on the ground off the skis. Larger baskets will be better for deeper snow and smaller baskets are fine if the snow cover is lighter.

The most important thing, no matter what kind of skis, bindings or poles you opt for, is to make sure your equipment, particularly your boots, fit you properly. Good boots will keep you warm and not cause blisters; skis that are suitable for your weight with a pack on will make your traveling easier; poles of the right height will help you use your energy most efficiently. It's possible to just slap on any old pair and go, but skiing on equipment that is well-matched to your height and weight makes a huge difference.

Classic versus Touring Skis

The two main kinds of skis that you can use for winter travel are classic *(right)* and touring *(left)*.

Classic skis are narrower and stiffer than touring skis, and are best used on terrain that is wide open with minimal vegetation. They are great for trips that will involve a lot of lake crossing, for example, or for skiing into recreation areas that have track-setting or established trails. Touring skis are wider and more flexible than classic cross-country skis. The wider the ski, the more varied the terrain it will be able to handle, especially off-trail. Because they're fatter than classic skis, touring skis can be just as good as snowshoes for traversing areas where there isn't too much vegetation.

Waxable versus Waxless Skis

Both classic and touring skis come in waxable and waxless versions. Waxless skis have rough grooves or "fish scales" carved into the base of the ski in the section under your foot. These scales are designed to let your ski slide forward but not backward, providing the slight grip underfoot that waxable skis achieve with grip wax. Most experienced skiers consider waxless skis to be strictly for beginners, while others appreciate the convenience and are willing to give up a little bit of performance. When deciding between the two, consider the climate you will be skiing in. Waxing is difficult in weather that is changing frequently or when it's just barely below or hovering around freezing temperatures. These are the conditions where waxless skis really shine.

Waxing Cross-Country Skis

There are two basic kinds of ski wax: glide wax for the tips and tails and kick wax for the section under the binding.

Glide waxes only need to be applied every 15 to 30 miles (25 to 50 km) for optimal effect, and less often if you don't mind being less efficient. You should use glide wax even if you have waxless skis ("waxless" only means they don't need kick wax).

Kick waxes are applied in thin layers under the binding of a waxable ski to give you a moment of grip when you step down on your ski and push off with each stride. It's best to apply these in several layers, using a wax that is appropriate for the temperature and type of snow. It makes a difference to what wax you use, for example, if the snow is fresh or has been sitting around for a while. Harder waxes are generally used for colder conditions and softer waxes for warmer.

Waxing is a science all its own (there are whole books written on the subject), but don't be daunted by all there is to learn. You can quickly learn enough to do an effective waxing job for most conditions and get much greater control over your skiing experience.

Before you head out on skis for a winter camping trip, make sure you have a few day trips under your belt and feel comfortable with your equipment.

Waxless skis are convenient and easy to maintain but they do not glide as efficiently as a properly waxed pair of waxable skis, and they can be noisy on the snow, making a zip-zip-zip sound as you go.

Check around for waxing workshops, which are often run for free or very low cost at outdoor stores that sell cross-country skis.

Basic Technique Tips

Unlike snowshoeing technique, cross-country skiing technique could fill a whole book. Still, your skill requirements from a winter camping perspective are fairly simple. You just need a decent kick-and-glide for flats, a bit of practice doing herringbone or side-stepping for ascents, and comfort "snowplowing" for descents. If you're new to cross-country skiing, I recommend that you take a few beginner lessons to learn efficient technique and develop confidence about basic waxing.

If you're a more experienced skier who has simply never used cross-country skis for a winter camping trip, keep in mind that all the extra weight you'll be transporting will change your technique a bit. Going uphill is more work with a pack, but is manageable if you get your waxing right. The extra weight on your back when you come down will make descents fast and exciting, so be ready to do some extra braking if you aren't comfortable flying down hills!

Getting Around in the Mountains

Winter backpacking in the mountains can be exhilarating, spectacular and challenging. However, there are a number of important technical and safety factors to be aware of before taking your backpack into the mountains.

The most common way to get around in the mountains in winter is on backcountry skis: either telemark or alpine touring (AT) skis, although snowshoes can also be used where the terrain is not too steep. Here we will focus on getting around in the mountains on skis.

If you go off established trails on either classic or touring skis, breaking trail will slow you down quite a bit, so be sure to factor that into your travel time. However, if everyone in your group takes turns leading, you'll all enjoy the benefit of sliding along easily in the track set down by the first person.

IMPORTANT

If you decide to venture into the rewarding world of winter mountain travel there are a number of risk factors to take into account. Traveling in mountainous terrain necessarily means that you'll be in more remote areas where any rescue attempt, if needed, will likely take a long time. For this reason it is critical to be totally self-sufficient both in terms of the equipment, clothing, and food you bring, as well as in the knowledge you possess to keep yourself and others in your party safe.

Mountain Trip Planning

There are some excellent books and online resources on how to properly plan for a successful winter mountain adventure, which I recommend consulting before doing your first trip. In addition to bringing the appropriate clothing, food, and equipment, your navigational equipment will be among the most important supplies you'll bring, and should be brought on every foray into the mountains—no matter how short. This is particularly important in the winter because of varied weather, complex topography, and a general absence of trails. Navigational equipment includes topographical maps of the area at a scale no less detailed than 1:50,000, compass, GPS, and, importantly, the ability to use these tools with confidence. Carry your topo maps folded in a sealable plastic bag (Ziploc-type bags work well) to protect them from moisture. Make sure at least one reliable person (who is not going on the trip) is aware of exactly where you are going and when to expect you back.

Mountain Weather

Mountain environments are notorious for "making their own weather" due to the varied topography that creates unpredictable precipitation, winds and storms. You must always be prepared to handle a wide variety of weather scenarios regardless of what the forecast says—it is nearly impossible to accurately forecast mountain weather. When heading to your destination in the mountains you will likely be ascending in elevation, so keep in mind that there is a temperature drop of approximately 11°F (6°C) for every 3000 feet (1,000 meters) of elevation gained. Combine this with the knowledge that night temperatures are colder than daytime temperatures, and this means that you need to be prepared for very cold temperatures when sleeping outside in the mountains. Bring a good quality down or synthetic sleeping bag rated to at least −4°F (−20°C) or colder. A synthetic outer bag is an inexpensive way to boost the temperature rating of your sleeping bag, if you're worried about being cold.

Special Clothing Considerations

Mountain weather is extremely variable. Over the course of one day you can experience everything from a scorching hot, sun-soaked alpine bowl to howling winds, blowing snow, and a blisteringly cold night. Gaining lots of elevation with the combined weight of a pack, skis and boots is sweaty work, but you'll cool down quickly as soon as you stop for a break. In these harsh and uncertain circumstances it is extra-important to have your clothing layering system dialed, making sure to wear wool and synthetic fibers and never cotton. Consider the sample clothing list in Chapter 1 as a minimum for camping in the mountains.

Sun protection is critically important in the mountains. The higher you get in altitude the less UV protection you'll be getting from the atmosphere, and you'll be getting the rays reflected from the snow as well. Bring a sunhat with good coverage, sun block of SPF 15 or higher, and dark, full-protection sunglasses that will minimize intense glare from the sun.

Avalanches

When you combine mountainous topography with winter weather conditions you automatically get the very real and deadly possibility of avalanches. Doubtless the biggest fear of any backcountry skier is that of being caught in an avalanche, and for good reason—approximately 25 people in the U.S. and 14 people in Canada die each year in avalanches.

Indications that you are entering an avalanche-prone area are not always so obvious. Proper training is your only defense.

The good news is that although not all avalanche accidents are foreseeable, many can be avoided with proper trip preparation and knowledge. This knowledge includes the ability to recognize and avoid avalanche terrain, the ability to assess snow stability, as well as being skilled in backcountry search and rescue techniques in case your party is involved in an avalanche.

So how does one learn these critical safety skills? The best way is to take an avalanche skills training course. Through organizations like the American Institute for Avalanche Research and Education (AIARE) and the Canadian Avalanche Association you can find courses regularly throughout the ski season, and they involve some classroom time as well as at least one full training day in the field. If you are planning to do any amount of backcountry travel this is the best safety preparation you can get, and it will be worth every penny.

Take a course, and ensure others on your trip have some training and experience as well. You should never be the only person on a trip with avalanche safety skills and equipment. If you are planning to go into a mountain area that you're not familiar with, watch the weather for that area for a few weeks before you go, and talk with locals who are familiar with recent snow conditions.

If you aren't able to take an avalanche skills training course before your trip, the next safest option is to do your trip with people very experienced and knowledgeable in winter mountain travel. Make sure their attitudes towards acceptable risks agree with your own—you'll be putting a lot of trust in them to make safe decisions. To boost your knowledge there are some excellent books written about avalanches, which may be helpful in learning some of the basics. Again, this is no substitute for a course, which, along with cautiously building up your own experience-based knowledge over a lifetime of mountain adventures, is the best option to keep you safe.

Backcountry Skiing and Snowboarding

Backcountry ski equipment is made for descending steep mountain slopes and more closely resembles downhill gear than cross-country. Telemarking and alpine touring (AT) are the two main styles of backcountry skiing, although snowboarding has increased in popularity as well with the development of splitboards.

What these types of travel all have in common is that they use the same method to ascend steep mountain slopes: skinning. Skins, named because of their origin as strips of sealskin, are strips of synthetic fabric with directional fibers on one side that allow the ski to glide forward but not slip back. Skins give the skier excellent traction on steep snow, allowing them to climb much steeper slopes than they could with wax or fish scales.

Telemark Skiing

Telemarking is the old-school, classic style of skiing with free heels. This style involves lifting the heel and dropping the knee of the inside ski, and leading with the outside ski to guide the skier through the turn.

Telemark equipment has evolved substantially over the past few decades. In the early days telemark skiers wore ankle-high leather boots with three-pin bindings and used long, skinny, wooden Nordic skis. Nowadays you can still buy leather boots and skinny skis (metal-edged), which some traditionalists prefer, but most telemarkers are at the other end of the spectrum using sturdy plastic boots, similar to downhill boots, and shaped skis suited to carving tight turns through steep powder. All telemark equipment shares the common elements of an attachment point to the ski at the boot's toe and some kind of cable or spring tensioning system that allows the heel to lift off the ski.

Learning to telemark ski is not easy, though. It requires a combination of balance and coordination that most people—even seasoned alpine skiers—take a while to master. If this style of skiing appeals to you then you'll find the rewards of learning to "tele" to be well worth the extra effort. The best way to learn is to take a lesson at a hill, or get tips from a friend who knows how to do it, and just start doing it. And don't be afraid to fall!

Alpine Touring

Alpine touring (AT) is essentially downhill skiing adapted for touring. AT skis use a binding that allows the heel to be free while ascending, and to lock in like a downhill binding for the descent. AT skiing is easier than telemarking and more versatile when skiing in challenging snow conditions such as wind-crusted or very wet snow.

AT skiing used to be the less-preferred form of backcountry skiing because the equipment was essentially modified downhill ski equipment, and therefore very heavy. AT equipment has gotten much lighter (especially the bindings), while telemark equipment has gotten more robust (and therefore heavier), so now the choice between these two of skiing is now purely a matter of style.

When performed well, telemarking is a very graceful, fluid way of skiing—a joy to do if you're good at it, and a joy to watch if you're not.

Snowboarding

Snowboarding is another option for getting around in the backcountry. A splitboard is a snowboard adapted to backcountry travel. For ascending the board can be split in two and the bindings rotated so that they resemble short, wide skis. Climbing skins are available to fit splitboards in their ascending format. The boards are joined together with latches for the descent.

Special Equipment for Backcountry Skiing

Backcountry skiing is one of the most equipment-intensive winter sports, partly due to the expensive safety equipment that is required. If you are planning to buy all your equipment new you can easily spend upwards of several thousand dollars just to get started. A more cost effective way to enter the sport is to rent your safety equipment for each outing and buy used skis, boots and poles. Safety equipment is not the place to cut corners on cost—this is the stuff that might save your life, if you and the people you are with know how to use it.

• **Skis** The type of ski you buy (its length, width, shape, and flex) will depend on your size and the type of skier you are. Get advice from a good ski shop on the best type of ski for you. Although there are skis marketed to AT and telemarking specifically, the differences are subtle. The most important thing is to get a ski that works for you.

• **Bindings** There's a wide range of options for both telemark and AT bindings. For telemark bindings, things to consider include flexibility, whether the tension is adjustable, and the weight of the binding. For AT bindings, consider whether you want a Dynafit or step-in type, what boot types fit it (not all bindings fit all boots), release mechanism, and weight.

• **Boots** There are many options for both telemark and AT boots, but the most important thing is how well the boot fits you. Lighter, more flexible boots are generally more comfortable and are suited for touring, whereas more rigid boots with a high cut and more buckles are designed for aggressive descents in steep terrain.

• **Poles** A pair of downhill ski poles that fit you and have baskets and wrist straps will do. You can spend more money to get lighter poles, or poles that are adjustable and can be modified into an emergency avalanche probe.

• **Skins** Climbing skins attach with a hook to the ski tip and stick to the base of the ski with special adhesive. When you are ready to descend, they can be easily peeled off and folded with their sticky sides together. You may need to trim your skins to fit your skis if they have a lot of shape. This is easily done with the tool that usually comes with any new set of wide skins.

• **Shovel** A must for every backcountry winter trip, a shovel can be used for digging out avalanche victims and making pits to test snow stability. Shovels are available that are

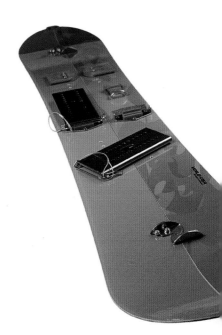

Splitboards offer backcountry travelers a great option for ascending. The alternative is to use snowshoes for the ascent, lugging the snowboard up on a backpack.

Climbing skins come in a variety of designs and price ranges. Just make sure you get ones that fit your skis properly.

lightweight, strong, and have removable handles for ease of packing. Choose according to price, weight, and how comfortable it is to hold.

• **Probe** Used to locate buried avalanche victims, a probe is another critical piece of lightweight and collapsible safety equipment. Probes are measured in centimeters and vary slightly in length from around 2.5 to 3.5 yards (240 to 320 cm), fully extended. It doesn't much matter what length you get as long as you have one.

• **Transceiver** Also called an avalanche beacon, a transceiver is what enables you to be found or to find someone buried in an avalanche, and is a must for every member of your party. Transceivers are battery powered and have two settings: "send" (sending signal, used while skiing), and "search" (used to search for avalanche victims wearing transceivers). Cost varies among brands, but they are all expensive. Get one that you find user-friendly in search mode—some are more sophisticated than others. Test your batteries before each trip, and bring an extra set just in case.

• **Repair Kit** Another essential item, but the contents will vary depending on the length and nature of your trip: extra boot strap, multi-tool, wire for repairing broken bindings, duct tape, pole basket, etc. This is not an exhaustive list—build a repair kit according to the equipment you are bringing, and the length of your trip.

Skijoring

Want to have all the fun of skiing with hardly any of the work? Skijoring is the way to go!

Skijoring involves connecting a person on cross-country skis to a dog via a harness. The dog pulls the person, usually with some assistance from the skier. Sometimes two or three dogs can be used, in which case the skier can be pulled very quickly and no kicking is necessary—the main concern becomes how to slow down! The easiest and quickest way to teach a dog to pull is by taking it out and having it pull with another dog who already knows how to do it. There are also some great books and online resources that offer tips on teaching dogs and their owners how to skijor. Many dogs love skijoring and enjoy it as an athletic activity to do with their human companion.

Equipment

Skis, Boots & Poles The same ski equipment that you would use for cross-country skiing.

Harness Buy a harness specific to skijoring. The harness has several parts:

• Wide, padded waist band to go around the skier.
• Dog harness that goes around the dog's front paws and chest so that the dog is pulling with the whole body, not the neck.
• Strong connector cord to go between skier and dog that has a section of bungee cord for shock absorption.
• Quick-release mechanism that attaches your waist band to the cord.

Dog! Husky breeds such as Siberian husky and Alaskan malamute have a natural pulling instinct and are therefore obvious choices for skijoring. Any breed can do it though, as long as it has enough bulk to pull the weight of a person. A dog should be at least one year old before it is trained to pull so as not to strain its growing bones.

Dog Sledding

Dog sledding is a very interesting and fun way to get around. However, there is so much to know about managing and caring for dogs, the sleds and the gear that for most people, going with a reputable dogsled guiding company will give you the best experience for your time and money. Many places offer a range of dog sledding options from day trips to full-blown, multi-day adventures.

Many different breeds (and mixed-breeds) love to pull and can make excellent skijoring dogs.

WINTER CAMP

Ahhh. Finally you're at camp. Time to relax and process the events of the day, kick off the boots and maybe slip into a nice pair of synthetic- or down-filled booties. Well, almost. There are a few chores to take care of first.

If you're in a group, the first thing to do upon arrival is to check out everyone's situation. Hopefully everyone was able to get at least 2 quarts (2 liters) of fluids into themselves throughout the day—or better still, 3. Remember, the more hydrated you are, the better your body and mind will function, and you will stay a lot warmer. If you are in a group, one person should get a few pots of water boiling while the rest set up camp. This way, everyone can have hot drinks as soon as camp is set up.

The Camp Triangle

The basic camp triangle concept: don't cook where you sleep, and don't poop where you eat.

The next thing to do is to plan the layout of your camp before you start putting up tents and setting up a cooking area. The traditional method for laying out a campsite is the "camp triangle," which suggests that you should separate the three main components of a camp—kitchen, bedroom and bathroom—in the corners of a triangle with at least 100 feet (30 meters) between each of them.

The triangle concept makes sense but you can bend the rules in the winter when it's cold and snowy and wildlife are less likely to be getting into your food. You still want your

Chapter 5

The Camp Triangle

Shelters

Setting Up Your Bed

The Camp Kitchen

Building a Fire

The Camp Bathroom

Bedtime Routine

bathroom area well away from everything, but cooking and sleeping will often happen in the same area. The most important thing in the winter is a layout that's convenient and comfortable, so you don't waste energy and risk getting your dry clothes wet by moving around too much after you've set everything up.

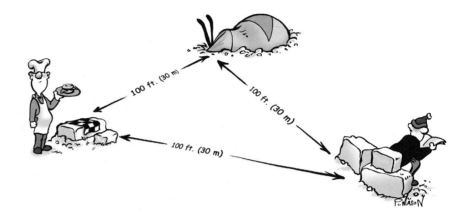

The basic camp triangle concept: don't cook where you sleep, and don't poop where you eat.

Shelters

Your next step setting up camp is creating some kind of shelter. There are many types of shelter you may use, tents being the most common. Other types of winter shelters include tarp shelters, quinzees, and various survival shelters such as lean-tos and tree well shelters.

Tents

A tent is a wonderful and simple shelter that will almost guarantee a good night out. A good tent is easy to set up, sheds rain and snow, blocks wind, and traps some of your body heat. The best kind of tent for winter camping is a four-season tent. These tents made specifically for mountaineering and winter camping are built for strength and warmth. Three-season tents, which are most common, have mesh walls and doors for weight-saving and airflow. Four-season tents have nylon walls which reduce drafts and retain more heat. They also usually have two doors and large vestibules where you can store extra gear or even use as a place to cook if the weather is bad.

How to Set Up Your Tent

1. Choose an area that is protected from the wind, tucked behind a knoll or a grove of trees.

2. In other seasons you would look for high ground to stay dry, but in the winter this may not be necessary. Just make sure there isn't any wet, unfrozen ground where you want to set up, and that there's no chance of rain or sleet in the forecast.

Like your sleeping bag, the life of your tent can be lengthened by storing it out of its stuff sack in a dry place out of direct sunlight when not in use. Threading it through a plastic hanger and hanging it in your gear closet will help prevent any moisture that may be trapped in the material from causing mold that can break down the fabric.

3. Look around for potential overhead hazards such as dead, rotten trees or loose branches that could come down in windy weather.

4. Using your snow shovel, dig out a square or rectangular box for your tent to sit in. If possible, orient it so that the smallest end of your tent is facing into the wind. You want to expose as little surface area to the wind as possible, and also prevent your fly from sticking to the sidewalls of your tent, which could cause excess condensation to build up inside.

Packing down the snow as a foundation for your tent helps prevent lumpy spots and ensure a comfortable sleep.

Spray paint your winter tent pegs a bright color so that they will be easy to find in the snow. You still might find that regular tent pegs are insufficient and too easily lost in winter conditions. Another option is to stick your skis or snowshoes and your poles in the snow and tie your tent lines to them. You can also tie your tent lines around a thick stick and bury it in the snow for a real bomber tie-down! Any anchor that you make by burying something in the snow is called a "dead man."

5. Use all of the snow that you excavate to either build the side walls of your box higher, which will provide some insulation and protection from the elements, or do what I do—pile all of the excavated snow where your vestibule door will be, where it can be used later to create a masterpiece of a kitchen!

6. Keeping your snowshoes or skis on, stomp down the snow inside your tent box to create a nice, even platform. Keep your snowshoes on until your sleeping bag is laid out and all your gear is in the tent. You don't want to step on the sleeping or tent platform with your snow boots; you will put big uncomfortable holes in the snow and hate yourself when you are trying to get comfortable at night.

7. If one side of the platform is higher than the other, this will be the best spot to have your head when you sleep.

8. Peg out all of the guy lines on your tent to increase the security of the tent in foul weather and increase the ventilation inside the fly, which will help reduce condensation.

Bivy Bags

A bivy bag, short for "bivouac bag," is a waterproof sack that fits around your sleeping bag to provide the bare minimalist form of shelter. Bivy bags were originally used by mountaineers who would carry them for emergencies in case they were forced to spend a night out on a route with no tent.

Tie a loop or two in the middle of the rope (using an alpine butterfly knot) and you can attach something useful, like a lantern.

Unless you're really hard core, you won't use a bivy bag as a form of shelter by itself, but rather as a complement to your sleeping system, particularly if you're sleeping in a snow shelter, lean-to or tarp shelter and need to protect your sleeping bag from the snow. A bivy acts like a shell layer for your sleeping system. It protects you from outside moisture and drafts and adds a few degrees of warmth.

The most expensive bivy bags are made of Gore-Tex or a similar material. But even the most breathable material will allow condensation to build up on the inside, so you should use a bivy in combination with one of the moisture-fighting measures outlined in Chapter 1, such as an overbag or vapor-barrier liner (VBL). If you sleep in a VBL, you don't need to worry about condensation in your bivy and can get away with a cheaper, less breathable material.

Because they just weigh a couple of pounds, you can carry your bivy bag as a piece of survival gear on day trips. If someone gets injured or you get stuck somewhere, you have a big waterproof, windproof shell to crawl into for extra warmth.

Covering the sides of the tarp with snow and building snow walls at the ends helps keep the wind out of your tarp shelter.

Tarp Shelters

The tarp shelter is a simple, effective and cheap shelter that is a favorite of mine for winter camping. All you need to build a tarp shelter is a tarp large enough to cover the length and width of your body, one long piece of rope or parachute cord (I always carry a 15-foot (5 m) length of 3-millimeter cord), some basic knots, sticks, and your imagination.

Built properly, a tarp shelter can protect you from the elements just as well as a tent. It will keep out precipitation, shield you from wind, reflect back some of your heat, and vent out moisture that in a tent would condense onto the walls and fall back onto you.

The ways of building a tarp shelter are limited only by your imagination. You can get really fancy and fine-tune the perfect cozy nesting area! Here is just one way to do it.

How to Construct a Tarp Shelter

1. Find two healthy, stable trees wide enough apart that you can lie stretched out between them.

2. Dig out and stomp down a rectangular sleeping platform between the trees where you intend to sleep.

3. Using your 3-millimeter cord or rope, tie a taut line between the two trees at chest height. What I like to do is use a clove hitch knot to attach the rope to the first tree, and tie off the tail of the rope with half hitches. Then about halfway along the remaining rope, I tie an alpine butterfly so that when my shelter is set up, I can hang a lantern from it. Very close to the second tree, I tie another alpine butterfly so I can wrap the tail around the tree and then insert it in the loop of the alpine butterfly. Using the loop creates a mechanical advantage so that I can pull the rope taut between the trees. (You can also use a slip knot if you prefer.) Then I tie off the end with half hitches.

4. Drape your tarp over the top of the rope.

5. Peg the edges of the tarp out into the snow or tie off to other trees or shrubs nearby. You can use sticks, skis, snowshoes, poles or anything else you have.

6. Fold one end of the tarp closed (the end where your feet will be) and leave the entrance open.

7. Cover the sides and the back of the tarp closest to the ground with snow to make a nice seal to keep the wind out. If your side walls don't touch down to the snow, build up a snow wall around the outside of your tarp shelter.

8. Build up a wall in front of the entrance that will block any wind and that you can later use as a kitchen.

Quinzees

A quinzee is probably the warmest type of winter shelter by far. A quinzee is a snow shelter similar to an igloo, except that instead of building it with snow blocks, you hollow out a massive pile of snow. Snow may be cold, but it's an excellent insulator and shelters made out of it can retain a lot of heat. Quinzees make great emergency shelters, but they aren't only for emergencies. Many people would rather sleep in a quinzee than a tent because of the warmth and quiet.

Quinzees can be quite spacious compared to a tent and they don't take up any space in your backpack!

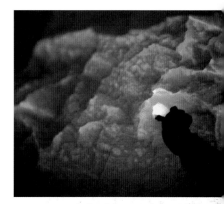

How to Construct a Quinzee

You can use any type of snow to build a quinzee. Follow these steps to build a luxurious quinzee for an overnight camping trip. To build an emergency quinzee, see the following section.

1. Stomp out a circle in the snow with a radius large enough to fit everyone who will sleep inside, allowing 1 foot (30 cm) for the thickness of the walls.

2. With whatever digging tools you have, shovel snow into a pile in the center of the circle. If you don't have a shovel, use snowshoes or the plastic insert from a backpack, or fill a tarp or tent fly by scooping snow onto it with your arms.

3. As your pile grows, pack it down. Use the end of a shovel, stand on it with your snowshoes, pat it with your hands. If there are two people, have one person shovel while the other packs. Packing helps to reduce the time it takes for the snow to firm up so you can dig it out. Packing is most important when the snow is very light and powdery.

4. Once the pile has reached the desired height and diameter (at least tall enough so that you can sit up in it) and you have given it a final pat down, collect a handful of sticks that are fairly skinny and about 2 feet (60 cm) long. Now take the sticks and plunge them sporadically into the snow pile, inserting in by about 12 inches (30 cm) at the base and tapering to 6 inches (15 cm) halfway up and 4 inches (10 cm) near the top. This marks the thickness of the walls, which should be about a foot thick at the base and 4 inches at the top. (The thinner snow at the top is so that if the ceiling collapses, you won't suffocate.) Now the pile of snow should look like a white porcupine.

5. Wait for the snow to settle and solidify before you attempt to dig it out. Snow that is very fluffy may take a few hours, whereas moist packing snow will probably be ready to dig out right away.

6. Once the snow pile is firm and settled, start excavating! First take note of the wind direction and start digging the door on the opposite side. Try to keep the entrance as small as possible, just big enough to slide in. If there's enough snow and time permits, immediately dig up a foot and then dig in again so you can have an elevated platform inside that is level with the top of the door. This creates what's called a cold air sink. All of the warm air from your body will stay above the platform and the cold air will sink down to the door.

7. As you are removing snow from the inside, watch for the sticks that you plunged in. Stop digging wherever you see the end of a stick. The digging seems tedious at first, but goes a lot quicker once your body is inside. I like to use a pot or a pot lid to dig, carve and shape out the inside of my quinzees.

8. Once the inside is hollowed out, construct your entrance by using all of the excavated snow to build a long wall on both sides of the path leading up to your door. This wall

A tarp lean-to makes a great addition to a campsite when the threat of rain or sleet is an issue, since it allows you to still enjoy time around the campfire as a group rather than hiding in your tents.

will act as a wind barrier, and if you feel like getting fancy, you can carve out one side and make your camp kitchen.

9. You can stuff your backpack and any other gear you don't need for the night into the opening of your quinzee. This works well as a door, keeping the heat in and the cold out.

10. Make sure to put in a few ventilation holes into the sides of your quinzee to let fresh air come in and moisture escape.

How to Construct an Emergency Quinzee

If you are caught out unexpected, you won't want to prepare such an elaborate structure as the one described above. Instead, scale down the size for one body or a very snug two bodies to keep as warm as possible. Speed up the process and reduce the amount of snow you need by filling the center with anything else you can find—logs, sticks, evergreen boughs (as many as possible, because you can use them later as a mattress), and even gear you do not need right away. Then cover the pile with snow to the size you want and let it sit for about an hour. After the snow has consolidated, pick a spot out of the wind to dig your entrance. Gently pull out the things you piled in the middle one by one, shaping and hollowing out the inside as you go.

Lean-Tos

There are a few other shelter types that are used primarily in survival situations, but which you may also want to try out for fun. They can be remarkably comfortable and warm if you build them well.

One of these shelters is the lean-to, a survival shelter that involves cobbling together materials at hand, such as branches and boughs, into a tent-like structure with an open front. There are many ways to build a lean-to and which one you choose depends on your imagination and the materials at hand.

How to Construct a Lean-To

A lean-to usually has an open side so that you can build a fire in front of it. If you find a boulder or cliff, build your open side facing the rock so that it will protect you from the wind and reflect the heat of the fire. You can also build a lean-to using a tarp, if you have one, in combination with natural materials.

1. To start, look for a fallen tree, a hollow near a tree stump or a big boulder—anywhere that offers some natural shelter to get you started.

2. From there you can start piling trees or sticks to create a framework for a roof and walls. If you have some rope or parachute cord, you can tie a small log between two trees to use as the apex of an A-frame. Then you can use sticks, branches, evergreen boughs and snow to fill in the side walls.

Coffin Shelters

A coffin shelter is the simplest shelter imaginable—a hole in the snow!

How to Construct a Coffin Shelter

1. Find an area with deep snow, that is protected from the wind, and, ideally, slightly elevated. Cold air sinks, so avoid valleys.

2. Dig out an area 3 to 4 feet deep that is a little longer than your body and slightly wider than your shoulders (roughly the dimensions of a coffin.)

3. Create a frame over the coffin by laying branches, poles, skis, snowshoes, or anything else available across the top. Put a roof on the shelter by laying a tarp or a cut-open garbage bag over the frame. Leave a 1-foot opening at one end for fresh air. Pile snow along the edges of the roofing to keep it down and keep drafts out. To create a peaked roof that will help shed snow, prop up a branch (or something similar) at each end of the coffin, and then tie a boot lace or piece of rope between the two. Your roof of choice then drapes over top. If you don't have a tarp or plastic to enclose your coffin, you can also use branches and evergreen boughs.

Drift Trenches

The drift trench or trench shelter is a shelter for an area where there's isn't enough snow to dig a coffin shelter or a quinzee, nor enough wood to build another kind of shelter.

Look around for areas where snow has accumulated and find the largest snowdrift you can. Then build the best possible shelter with the available snow. For example, if you find a small drift, dig the deepest coffin shelter you can, as described above; if you find a big drift, dig into the side of it and make a quinzee. This is the same as digging a normal quinzee, but better because you don't have to waste any energy building a snow pile. If there are no sticks to plunge into the drift as a guide for thickness, use anything you have like skis and ski poles, or judge thickness by the amount of light coming through.

Snow Caves

If you are in a mountainous area or an area with very deep snow and a steep hillside, you might be fortunate enough to be able to dig yourself a snow cave in the side of the hill. Similar to a quinzee, this is a great time- and energy-saving shelter that doesn't require you to pile snow and wait for it to firm up.

Tree Well Shelters

Tree well shelters are great shelters that form naturally in deep snow below evergreen trees with branches that are thick and low enough to block snow accumulation near their trunks. Just climb into the hollow of the tree well and carve out a sleeping area. You will be protected on all sides by the snow and by the thick, green branches overhead.

Sick in a Tree Well Shelter

One winter, two buddies and I headed out to British Columbia from Ontario to go skiing in the mountains. Because we didn't have much money and were working with a $250 budget each, we took a Greyhound Bus. This mode of transportation amounted to 76 hours of travel each way, but it only cost $200 round-trip, taxes included.

Unfortunately, I must have caught some kind of bug along the way because I became very ill on our second day in the mountains, the first of what turned out to be the four sickest days of my life. I was weak, dizzy and had a pounding headache. All I wanted to do was lie down and rest. Being 18 years old at the time and hard-headed, I tried to tough it out at first, but soon I felt so weak that I had to conclude that my skiing adventure was over for now. I'd left home with no credit or debit card, and had only $50 on me, so there was no hope of heading back to civilization and landing a warm, dry bed in a motel for a few days.

However, snow and trees were abundantly available, so I decided to use my remaining energy to make my own little mountain hostel. I optimistically assured my buddies that I'd be alright and encouraged them to continue on to the alpine valley where we had planned to camp, so that they could spend the next few days skiing. I'd just rest for a bit and join them for a few runs when I felt better. Looking back, this decision seems incredibly foolish because if I hadn't been as lucky as I was, I could have wound up dead.

As it was, I skied off to one side of the mountain into a heavily wooded area. With no tent or tarp, my best option was to build a tree well shelter. I remember standing there exhausted for quite some time just staring out at the mountains, feeling hugely disappointed that I wouldn't be skiing, and wondering if I'd even have the energy to dig down into the snow. I found a good tree and started digging. It turned out to be a great shelter, about five feet deep and just a little longer then my body, twice my width and nicely squared out. The branches above made a perfect canopy and sheltered me from falling snow, while the snow walls provided good insulation from the cold and protection from the wind. By the time it was done, I was completely wiped out and ready to collapse.

I ended up spending two days in that shelter by myself. I set up my stove next to me and was mindful to eat and drink what I could to stay hydrated and nourished despite having no appetite. I don't think I have ever been so lonely. For company, all I had was a tattered old copy of a mountain biking magazine... and the people who, in my fevered state, I kept imagining were there with me. It must have been a fairly high fever because throughout the first night in the tree well I was certain that someone was trying to give me white medicine on a spoon. I also believed for a while that there were some folks in the shelter who wanted me to guide them off the mountain. I remember trying to convince them that I was too sick and weak to do so, and explaining to them that it was easy enough for them to make their way down on their own if they'd let me describe the route for them.

Finally I decided that it was best to leave the shelter, leave a message for my buddies in the village, and see if I could get on a bus home. On my way down the mountain, I fell neck-deep into another tree well, which in my weakened state took a lot of my energy to climb out of. With grim determination, I eventually made it back to safety. Once on the bus, with more sleep and lots of water, I started to feel a bit better. I ended up spending 152 hours on a bus to cross the country, ski for one day and feel like I was dying alone in a snow pit for two, but it was still a great adventure and I learned a lot about taking care of myself in emergency situations and the importance of proper planning. I even made it home with some spare change left in my pockets!

Lofting and shaking the sleeping bag ensures that your insulation is evenly distributed and fluffed up to be as warm as possible.

Setting Up Your Bed

After setting up your shelter, set up your sleeping system before you move on to other tasks. First lay out your closed-cell foam pad or inflatable pad. If you are going to use both for extra insulation, put the closed-cell foam pad on top. This provides the warmest combination by putting the densest insulation closest to your body. You'll still feel the comfort of the air pad underneath.

Next lay out your sleeping bag on top of your mattress. When you take your sleeping bag out of its stuff sack it will be flat, so you need to manually "loft" it. Grab the sleeping bag from the hood and shake it up and down in a wave-like motion. Then grab hold of the top and the bottom of the zipper and shake the bag to one side, repeating the same process on the non-zipper side.

Put any clothing you plan to sleep in inside the sleeping bag. Find your headlamp and tuck it into your pocket so you'll be ready for dark. Put your book and toothbrush and toothpaste in the side pocket of your tent.

Get your dry clothes, socks and footwear ready to put on. Unless it's an emergency and you're almost hypothermic, save these dry clothes until you've finished the hard work of setting up camp and built your kitchen. You've already worked all day in the clothes you are wearing so you might as well finish up the day's work in them as well. You don't want to run the chance of getting any moisture in your dry clothes.

Once everything is laid out and organized, you can relax and enjoy dinner and hanging out around the fire. At bedtime, all you have to do is take off your boots and clothes and slip into your bag—yee-haw!

The Camp Kitchen

Aside from the seven to nine hours sleeping in your shelter, you'll spend the rest of your time hanging out in camp cooking and boiling water. To cook and boil water, you've got to have a kitchen—an awesome, convenient and comfortable kitchen with room for a friend or two for company!

Just like at home, counter space is a valuable asset, but with snow as your building material, custom features like cup and utensil holders become very affordable.

Get around to building your kitchen sooner rather than later so that it has time to settle in the sun. By early evening your kitchen counter will be stronger and more sturdy.

Sleeping pad chairs are a treat when you want to relax, but if you are trying to save space in your backpack, you can always carve a throne out of the snow and line it with your sleeping pad.

Lay a square piece of a closed-cell foam pad (the thicker the better) on the ground in front of your kitchen platform to stand on. It's hard to keep your feet warm when you're just standing around, and this will cut the heat loss considerably and keep your whole body warmer as a result.

When I'm camping alone or with a couple of people, I like to have my kitchen right outside the front door of my tent vestibule or shelter entrance. In the winter you need to keep all your essentials very organized and close at hand, and it doesn't get any more cozy or convenient than this. If you have dug out your shelter properly and piled all of the snow in front of your door, you should have plenty of snow to carve out a nice kitchen area.

If you are camping in a larger group, make a separate communal kitchen in the center of your camp where you can all cook together. Follow the same procedure outlined below, but double or triple the size, making sure you have enough space to move around without bumping into each other and potentially dumping precious pots of food and water.

How to Build a Snow Kitchen

1. Using a shovel or snowshoes, build up a snow bank that's between waist and chest height to use as a kitchen counter. You'll be spending a lot of time cooking, so build a it tall enough so you can work comfortably without doing a lot of bending over.

2. Compact and carve the snow into a rectangle with a solid, flat tabletop. Make sure to compress the side walls so that the whole platform is solid and stable.

3. Once your platform is perfectly shaped, customize and add any features you can think of to create the ultimate kitchen. Here are some suggestions:

   - Lightly kick a toe box at the bottom of your kitchen platform for your toes to slide under, so you can stand closer to your counter without bending over.

   - Push your water bottles into the countertop to make hands-free water bottle holders for pouring hot water. Make holders for your coffee mug and fuel bottle too.

   - Chisel out a shallow round circle for your heat reflector, stove and windscreen to prevent them from sliding around when you're cooking. Sometimes the stove will melt the snow and make it icy and slippery.

   - Create two or three slots beside the stove for your utensils to stand upright in.

   - On one side of your countertop, carve out a square box to store miscellaneous kitchen items. This keeps things from blowing away or getting lost in the snow.

   - On the other side of your cooking platform, clear a space that you can keep full of snow blocks or clean snow for boiling drinking water.

4. Don't forget to carve yourself a throne to relax in while you're cooking or melting water. Fit your throne with a foam pad for insulation to keep your butt warm while you lounge.

5. Organize and lay out all of your kitchen gear and you are set for the night and the next morning.

Dishwashing

Washing dishes in the winter can be a bit of a pain. Personally, I like to avoid doing dishes altogether so that I don't have to waste time, energy and fuel melting snow to make dishwater, although you can if you like. I can usually get my mug or bowl clean enough by licking the food out and chasing my meal with a hot drink, swishing it around to clean out any food particles.

For easy pot scrubbing, clean out your pot with your spoon as thoroughly as possible, leaving no chunks of food behind, then pack the pot full of snow (coarse corn or granular snow works best). Let the snow sit until the pot is super cold. Push down on the snow in the pot and twist it back and forth to scour the inside of the pot. Almost all of the food residue should now be on the snow block and ready to discard into the bushes, leaving your pot clean and ready for another meal. Remaining frozen food can be scraped out, swished out with a bit of hot water, or left in the pot to add to your next meal or mix in with the hot water when you melt snow for drinking!

Building a Fire

Your file will be a valuable source of warmth, a way to dry out gear, and an alternate heat source for cooking. You need top-notch campfire lighting skills to be warm and comfortable in the winter. Keep in mind that every fire needs three things to burn: heat, fuel and oxygen. The heat comes from your ignition source (lighter or matches), the fuel is your wood of varying sizes, and the oxygen comes from building your fire in a way that lets air flow around the fuel.

Buy wooden strike-anywhere matches and waterproof them by dipping the ends in hot paraffin wax; then store them in a watertight container or Ziploc baggie.

Ignition

The heat part of the equation starts with a flame. Use a plastic lighter or matches. If you are fond of matches, use the wooden "strike anywhere" variety. Paper matches are flimsy, and any kind of "safety" match is less convenient (and less safe in the wilderness!) because it requires you to have a dry match package to strike it on. I personally always pack a couple of plastic lighters (in case I lose one) as well as a small stash of waterproofed, strike-anywhere matches—two fire lighting methods are better than one.

You can speed up the ignition process by using a candle to dry out your tinder, or using fire-starting sticks or magnesium fire starter. Hone your skills so that you don't have to rely on these aids too much, so that you have something to fall back on in emergencies.

Fuel

Collecting Firewood

Now that you have your heat source standing by, assemble your fuel by collecting a huge amount of wood suitable for burning. This means any dry wood (not rotten) such as sticks, branches, twigs and any half-burnt, dried-out stumps that you might happen to see. (These often have dry sap in them and are great for burning.)

Be careful to stay away from wood that is green or rubbery, which indicates that it is still alive. Green wood will often snap easily in the winter because it is frozen, but it will still be wet inside and just smoke a lot when you try to burn it.

Make sure to collect more wood than you think you'll need and to collect wood of varying sizes, from toothpick-sized twigs to baseball bat–sized branches and larger.

In the winter you will not generally have to worry about avoiding wood that has been soaked by rain, but if you're having trouble finding dry wood, look under the sheltered base of any evergreen tree.

Unless it's an absolute emergency, don't snap any branches or peel bark off any tree, dead or alive—this will create an eyesore in heavily used areas and can damage trees needlessly. Use fallen trees and branches exclusively if possible.

How to Build a Campfire

To build a fire that will light quickly and burn efficiently, use the campfire layering system. Build your fire in layers of increasing size, with small, fast-burning fuels on the bottom and heavy, slower-burning fuels on top.

1. First arrange your wood into four to five different piles from small to large so you can easily find fuel of the right size when you're tending your fire. Then you can start building your fire from the bottom up.

2. Your first layer should be your igniting layer, called tinder: birch bark, grass, paper or thin wood shavings—something that will light very easily, burn hot and fast and ignite the larger wood. I think birch bark is the best fire starter by far, even when wet.

If you can find some birch bark off a dead branch or on the ground, tear it up into thin strips and crumple the strips into balls.

3. The next layer should be small, dry twigs the size of toothpicks. Lay these lightly in multiple layers, increasing the size of sticks as you go, making each layer thick enough that it will burn long enough to ignite the next layer.

Also think about layering different types of wood as well as different thicknesses. Smaller, lower layers should be fast-burning softwood like cedar or balsam. Use hardwood for the higher, thicker layers once the fire gets going. Hardwood will ensure a long-lasting, very hot burn. Oak, maple, beech and ironwood are some great hardwoods to burn. Your goal is a nice hot bed of coals, something that will last a long time and throw off a lot of heat, and thick hardwoods will accomplish this best.

Styles of Fire Building

When you are layering your fire, you need to think about oxygen. If everything is packed together and there is no air flow through the layers, your fire won't burn efficiently. There are a couple of classic styles of fire layout that follow the campfire layering system and ensure plenty of airflow around the fuel. Most fires you build will be variations on these two types.

A tipi fire starts with a pile of tinder in the center, which is then surrounded by thin sticks to form a tipi. Once the tipi is burning strong, continue to add wood to the tipi until the fire is strong enough so that you can just pile wood on top.

The Tipi Fire

Put all of your paper or lighting material in the center of where your fire will be. Around this pile of tinder, stand up your first, thin layer of sticks like the poles of a tipi, leaning them against each other at the apex. Add thicker and thicker sticks to the tipi, building up to large pieces of hardwood. Light the tipi in the center. Once all of the wood has ignited, you can add more wood around the fire. Usually by this time the tipi will fall over and you can just toss wood on top since everything is now burning hot and efficiently.

The Log Home Fire

This method is similar to the tipi method, except that instead of building a tipi around your pile of tinder, you build a log cabin structure around it. This method works well for stacking bigger pieces of hardwood around the fire, and if the bigger wood is damp or wet, you can burn smaller wood inside of the cabin until the big pieces start burning.

If your wood is wet, light your fire with a candle—tea lights work well. Place the candle underneath your fire with lots of space around it for oxygen. The candle will dry your wood out and you should have no problem getting your fire going, saving matches and lighter fuel.

The Camp Bathroom

Winter camping makes going to the bathroom truly interesting. Depending on the conditions, it can even feel a little epic. But don't let the cold and snow tempt you to cut corners when it comes to backcountry sanitation. The fact that it's freezing cold and there's nobody else around is no excuse to get sloppy and abandon your "leave no trace" ethics. Think carefully about the springtime impact of any mess you leave behind.

First of all, it's a good idea to have a designated pee spot so people are not leaving yellow spots all over camp. You should kick snow over the spot each time you pee and make sure everything's hidden before you leave.

When it comes to taking care of business from the other end, there are a few options. Obviously, if you are camping in a spot that is busy enough in the summertime to have existing facilities—like pit toilets or backcountry "thunder boxes"—you should make every effort to use these. Otherwise, you should designate a general bathroom area far away from your sleeping and cooking area—and preferably downwind! Look for a place that is easy to walk to, sheltered for privacy, away from any summertime traffic areas like trails or campsites, and far away (at least 200 feet or 60 meters) from lakes and streams.

If the ground is unfrozen, you can bury your waste in the soil just like you would in the summertime, but otherwise you will be burying your waste in the snow, which means it will be resting on the surface when the snow melts. Try to find a site that is as thickly overgrown and as flat as possible to keep from polluting surface runoff.

Within this general bathroom area, each person should dig their own cat hole in the snow. Holes should be deep enough to fully cover the feces. When finished, the hole should be filled and marked with an upright stick so nobody else steps or tries digging in the same spot. Spacing out multiple cat holes in one general area has a smaller impact than if you were to dig one communal pit for everyone, allowing everything to break down a lot quicker in the spring.

When it comes to toilet paper, you're best to do without. Believe it or not, you can use snow for the ultimate winter camping experience. It really works—snow is made of water after all! Just pack yourself (if snow conditions permit) some nice egg-shaped snowballs. This is the most hard core way to do things, and, hey, winter camping is hard core!

If you choose to use toilet paper that's perfectly fine—we need to have some comforts—but you can't bury it in the snow. Animals will dig it up and there will be unsightly garbage floating around well into springtime. A better method is to put used toilet paper into a paper bag and then seal it in a plastic bag. You can then either pack the whole thing out or burn the paper bag in a roaring campfire.

To avoid embarrassing encounters in large groups, have one designated pathway to the latrine area and hang a roll of communal toilet paper on a stick near the path. When you go to the can, take this roll with you to signal that someone is "busy" over there.

Hygiene

Just because you are out on a winter camping trip doesn't mean you can totally forget about personal hygiene. Really, the most important thing is to always keep your hands clean, especially after you have used the facilities and anytime you are handling food or working in the kitchen.

In winter it's not always practical to heat up water to wash and rinse your hands. But we have been blessed with a beautiful product called hand sanitizer. This is an alcohol-based gel hand cleaner. You just squeeze a drop or two on your hands, rub them together until dry and, voilà! your hands are cleaner (or at least more germ-free) than if you had washed them with hot water and soap. Hand sanitizer evaporates and leaves no oily or creamy residue.

Hand sanitizer is made mostly of alcohol, which evaporates quickly, so be careful you don't freeze your hands—have your warm mitts ready to put on as soon as you're done.

Although the snowball might not be an attractive alternative to toilet paper, give it a try! Who knows, you might prefer it and find yourself installing a freezer in your ensuite.

Remember to wash your hands often or you could be sharing more than dried fruit with your buddies

Bedtime Routine

After you've got your camp set up, your bathroom organized, and your dinner cooked and cleaned up, the final step of your camp routine is getting ready for a warm night in bed. With your sleeping system all set up as outlined in Chapter 1, there are a few things you can do at this time that will help guarantee you a warmer sleep while also preparing you for the next day.

One hour before heading off to bed, you should stop drinking fluids so you won't have to pee during the night. But you should get water ready for the next day. Fire up your stove and boil enough water to fill one and a half water bottles. Fill up a water bottle right to the top and tighten the lid securely. Then toss the boiling hot water bottle into your sleeping bag (make sure there are no leaks and the bottle is dry). Fold the top of your sleeping bag to trap all of the heat inside. Leave the remaining water in the pot and put the lid on.

About 15 minutes before bed, fire up your stove again. Using the leftover water in the pot, start melting snow until you have enough to fill another water bottle. Boil the water and pour it into your second water bottle. Slip a clean, dry sock or insulating cover over the bottle and toss it into your sleeping bag with the other bottle.

Just before crawling into the old fart sack, stoke your own furnace by eating a fatty snack. Take a pee break. Now you're just about ready for bed. I find that most evenings my feet are fairly cold by bedtime and I might have a slight chill from hanging around camp. A good rule is "Go to bed warm, sleep warm." Running ferociously on the spot or doing 50 jumping jacks should be good enough to fire up your internal furnace. If you are really cold, take off your outer pant and coat shell and slip into your sleeping bag with all of your other layers on, then finish taking off the rest of your layers while zipped into your bag. I guarantee you that by the time you finish getting all of those layers off within the confines of your bag, you may be extremely frustrated but you will also be nice and warm!

Your sleeping bag should be very warm and inviting because of the two hot water bottles. The most inviting part of the day is slipping into your sleeping bag, getting all zipped in and wrapping your cold feet and toes around a warm water bottle!

The bottle that has been in your bag for over an hour should have cooled enough to hold against bare skin. The other bottle in the sock will continue to release heat throughout the night.

You can move your bottles around to heat yourself up wherever you want. Between your inner thighs is a good place—where your femoral artery passes near the surface and can distribute heat through your body—or your abdomen. Make sure to warm up all your extremities first, because this is where your core heat is lost first. If your feet, hands and head are warm, your core will be warmer.

The thick sock around the hot water bottle will help slow the release of heat from within so that you can get warmth from it throughout the night.

Take out your boot liners or foot beds and slide them into the bottom of your sleeping bag for the night. By morning they'll be warm and dry and you can start the day with happy feet. Also make sure that you fully loosen the laces of your boots, pull out the tongue and force the sides open before bed. If you don't, and you leave them out, the moisture from your feet will freeze by morning, making it difficult and uncomfortable to put your boots on.

NAVIGATION

You may not think about it too much, but you use navigation almost every day of your life. Navigation is simply the process of plotting and following a route from one place to another and knowing your position in relation to some familiar reference point, be it the coordinates on a map, a trailhead, or the grocery store down the street.

Chapter 6

The Compass

Topographic Maps

Magnetic North and Declination

Using a Map and Compass

In well-traveled areas like state, provincial and national parks, the only navigation skills you may need are how to read a basic trail map and follow signs. But in the winter when snow makes marked trails harder to follow (and off-trail exploration easier and more tempting) you'll want to know how to use a topographic map and a compass. A global positioning system (GPS) device can be a great navigational tool, but a GPS can always fail in the field and it's not a good substitute for map and compass skills.

Sometimes referred to as very expensive battery holders, GPS devices should only be used in conjunction with a map and compass.

Navigation with a map and compass is something you need to spend time to learn and practice often. It's a good idea to read this section, learn from a friend or better yet, take a course, and spend some time out in the field practicing using a map and compass in a familiar area before you decide to journey off into the woods by yourself. It can be very easy to get disoriented, turned around in circles and lost out in the bush, especially if you are not following a trail.

The Compass

A standard orienteering compass is all you need to take a bearing and then plot and follow a course in the wilderness. This type of compass has a clear base plate with scales on the side for measuring distances on maps and a big directional arrow pointing forward which is called the direction of travel arrow.

Fixed onto the base plate is a rotating ring, called an azimuth or bezel, with degrees and directions marked on it. The bezel is filled with a liquid and the magnetic needle floats inside this liquid, always pointing to magnetic north.

On the base of the bezel you'll see a big red arrow and a series of straight black lines called orienting lines or meridian lines. These lines and the arrow all move together when you rotate the bezel.

Underneath the outer ring of the bezel at the front is a stationary black line that sits beneath the rotating numbers. This is referred to as the index line, from which you can read your bearing, or heading, in degrees. Just as there are 360 degrees in a circle, there are 360 degrees marked on your compass.

You can buy a bare-bones orienteering compass for as little as 10 dollars. More expensive models come with bells and whistles like a sighting mirror, an adjustable declination screw, a magnifying glass, extra scales marked on the base plate or even a clinometer to measure the angle of a slope.

Sometimes referred to as very expensive battery holders, GPS devices should only be used in conjunction with a map and compass.

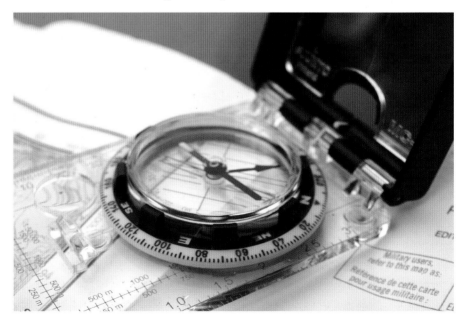

Topographic Maps

A topographic map, or "topo," is a two-dimensional representation of the earth's surface, showing geographical features such as lakes, rivers fields and forests, as well as topographic features like mountains, cliffs and hills. Topo maps have contour lines which join areas of equal elevation, and the spaces between the lines indicate a specific amount of elevation gain or loss, such as 50 feet. The closer the lines are together, the steeper the terrain.

Different land features are marked on the map using different colors and shading, while manmade structures such as buildings, bridges and roads are typically represented by symbols. A legend tells you what the different symbols and colors represent.

Distance is measured using a scale marked at the bottom of the map. Topo maps come in a variety of scales, such as 1:25,000 or 1:50,000. The smaller the number, the larger the scale of the map, meaning it shows greater detail over a smaller area. 1:50,000 is a good scale for navigating through the bush.

Topo maps usually have lines, called grid or UTM (universal transverse mercator) lines, running horizontally and vertically and dividing the map into squares. Depending on the scale of the map, these blue squares represent a certain measurement of area on the ground, and you can quickly estimate distance by counting grid squares.

The top of a topographic map points to true north—the direction of the North Pole. Grid lines pointing towards the top of the map point to grid north—which is almost the same as true north but varies slightly due to the difference between the straight lines of the grid and the curvature of the earth. Finally, there should be an arrow in the margin of the map that points to magnetic north, and you'll need to pay attention to this if you're going to use a compass with your map. This arrow and information recorded next to it is the declination diagram.

People who get used to reading topo maps can get really good at visualizing the terrain simply by looking at a map, and sometimes they can even navigate using the map alone.

Magnetic North and Declination

The magnetic pole isn't in the same place as the true North Pole, confusingly; it is a ways off to one side. So anytime you are using your compass, which points to magnetic north, together with your map, which is aligned with true north, you'll need to adjust for the difference. This angle of difference between the direction of magnetic north and the direction of true north is called magnetic declination.

Okay, there is one area on earth where true north and magnetic north are the same direction, and that is along the agonic line. This is an imaginary line that runs north to south and through both the true and magnetic north poles. In the northwest hemisphere the agonic line runs somewhere through western Lake Superior and Lake Michigan toward Florida and the Bahamas. If you are to the east of the agonic line you will have what is called a west declination because your compasses needle is pushed west of true north. If you are west of the agonic line you will have an east declination.

The degree of declination varies from place to place and from map to map—the further you are from the agonic line, the greater it will be. So you have to consult your map to find out what the declination is for your area. Maps usually have a declination diagram to give you this information.

To complicate matters further, the magnetic pole moves a little bit every year (and this is also why maps are aligned to true north and not magnetic north, in case you were wondering). So on the map where the declination is marked, there should also be a date and a note about annual variance. Often the annual variance will be negligible and you won't have to worry about it, but if the annual variance is significant and the map is old, you'll have to do some simple math to calculate the updated declination, multiplying the annual variance by the years that have passed and adjusting the declination accordingly.

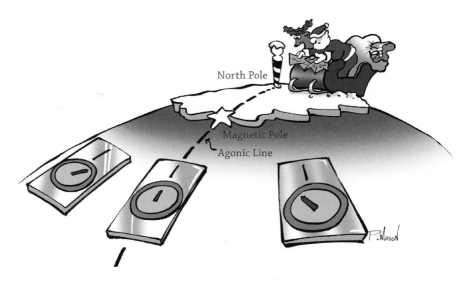

If you do not live along the agonic line you will have to adjust for magnetic declination when you are using a map and compass together.

Using a Map and Compass

How to Take a Bearing from a Map

This is how you take a compass bearing to get to a point on the map:

1. Find your known position on the map (point A). Then find the point on the map that you want to get to (point B).

2. Place the left edge of your compass base plate along the map so that it connects the

two points, making sure that the direction of travel arrow is pointing in the direction you wish to go. If the points are further apart than the length of your base plate, use something with a straight edge to draw a line between them, then place your base plate along that line.

3. Rotate the bezel until the orienting lines inside the bezel are parallel with the grid lines on the map, making sure your orienting arrow—the boxed arrow on the bottom of the bezel—is pointing towards grid north at the top of the map.

4. Now take a look at your index line and read the number above it. This is your bearing to grid north.

Just as important as making sure your stove is working correctly, you will want to inspect your compass to ensure it is in good working order well before you need to rely on it.

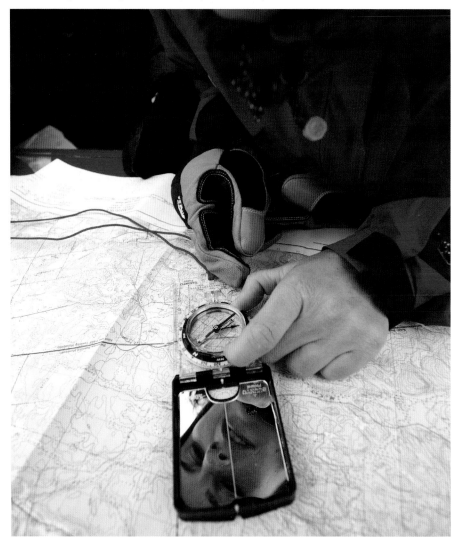

5. Remember that the compass needle will point to magnetic north, not grid north, so you will have to correct for the declination as described below. How you calculate for declination depends on whether you are west or east of the agonic line.

6. Now you should have your final bearing which you can follow in the field.

West vs East Declination

If you are not sure if you are east or west of the agonic line, check the declination diagram on your map. If the magnetic north arrow points to the left of true north, you are east of the agonic line. When you are east of the agonic line, you will add the degrees of declination to your bearing when going from map to compass. If the magnetic north arrow points to the right of true north, you are west of the agonic line. When you are west of the agonic line, you will subtract the degrees of declination from your bearing when going from map to compass.

When you are doing the opposite, and trying to figure out what direction you are already facing by looking at the map, when you are east of the agonic line you will subtract the degrees of declination from the compass reading you take in the field. When you are west of the agonic line you will add the degrees of declination to the compass reading you take in the field. This second method is covered in more detail in the section below on How to Plot a Bearing.

How to Follow a Bearing

Once you have your bearing from the map, follow this bearing to get where you want to go.

1. If it's not still set from the previous step, adjust the compass bezel to match the bearing you've calculated.

2. Hold the compass level in your hand in front of you and out at arm's length with the direction of travel arrow pointing forward.

3. Rotate your whole body until the red end of the needle is lined up exactly inside the boxed red arrow on your bezel. I like to call this "putting the red in the bed" and tell myself to "add the declination before putting the red in the bed."

4. The direction of the travel arrow, and your whole body, should now be facing the direction you need to go.

5. Before heading off on your bearing, take another look at your map and note any distinguishing natural features along your route. This will help you to stay on course.

6. You can't look at your compass all the time while you're walking, so look ahead of you and pick an obvious feature to walk towards. For example, if there is a big tree that stands out in the distance in line with your bearing, put away your compass and head straight for the tree. When you get to that tree, pull out your compass and repeat

If you do not hold your compass level (parallel with the ground) you will find the needle bobs around and you will not get an accurate reading. A good trick is to hold it steady right against your belly button.

the process. If you get into some thick bush, the features you pick may have to be very close together. Another method is to have a buddy walk away from you along the bearing until he gets out of view or off course; then you can catch up to him and repeat the process.

7. Keep checking your topographic map as you go and comparing it with the landscape.

How to Take a Bearing from the Field

Sometimes you may want to take a bearing towards something you can see in the field. An example is when you are headed towards a hill in the distance, but will have to walk through a thick forest to get there—you can take a bearing on the mountain while it's in sight, and then follow the bearing through the forest. Follow these steps:

1. Hold your compass level in your hand and up at eye level.

2. Point your sight line (direction of travel arrow) at the landmark you want to take a bearing to.

3. Keeping your hand steady and still pointing the sight line, turn the bezel with your fingers until the magnetic north needle is inside the boxed arrow on the bezel.

4. Take a look at your index line to read the number. This is your bearing.

5. You don't have to make any adjustment for declination because you're not working off a map.

How to Plot a Bearing

Drawing a bearing that you take in the field onto your map is called plotting. Sometimes you may want to plot your bearing to see what kind of topography you'll be traveling through or to measure the distance to your destination. To plot a bearing, follow these steps:

1. To go from the field to the map, you need to adjust for declination. Because you are taking a bearing from the field and applying it to the map, you do the opposite of what you did to go from map to field. If you have a west declination (the magnetic north arrow points to the left of true north in the declination diagram on the map), subtract the declination from your bearing. If you have an east declination (the magnetic north arrow points to the right of true north in the declination diagram on the map), add the declination to your bearing. Rotate the bezel to adjust for the new bearing.

2. Put a dot on the map to mark the place where you took your bearing from.

3. Line up the bottom left edge of your compass with the dot and then pivot your base plate until the orienting lines inside the bezel are parallel with the grid lines on the map, making sure your orienting arrow—the boxed arrow on the bottom of the

Not only does the compass cord help your compass double as a winter camping fashion accessory; it can also be used to measure distances on the map.

bezel—is pointing towards grid north at the top of the map.

4. Now you can draw a line along the left edge of your base plate from the location you are standing to the place you want to go. You have just plotted your bearing.

Aiming Off

Aiming off is essentially taking a bearing of where you wish to travel and purposely adding or subtracting a bunch of degrees to put you off course. For example, imagine that you want to get to Annie's gas station in the next nearest town to get supplies and it is 10 miles (16 km) away to the north. There is a road that runs for quite some distance in an east-west direction past the gas station. Imagine that you take a bearing from the map and discover that that if you walked in a perfectly straight line due North, you would end up at Annie's. However, the chances of being able to walk a perfectly straight line over such a distance is extremely difficult, and if you ended up slightly off, you'd have no idea whether you should head east or west when you hit the road. In this case, you'd intentionally aim off—say, 40 degrees off from your straight line bearing—so that when you eventually hit the country road, you know that you need to turn left and walk in a westward direction to make it to Annie's. Aiming off is a great technique to use when your destination is somewhere along a lake, stream, ridge line, trail road, or other linear feature.

Back Bearing

Also known as a reciprocal bearing, back bearing is used when you have been going in a straight line in one direction and want to return to where you started. To do so, add 180 degrees to that bearing and put the red in the bed. You'll turn right around in a half circle so that all you have to do is walk until you get back to where you came from.

Dead Reckoning

By using the following three examples you can determine approximately how much distance you have covered over a given amount of time, how much time it has taken you to cover a given distance and at what speed you have been moving over a given area. It's best to already have an idea of how long it takes you to travel a mile or kilometer on easy terrain with a pack on. You can do this by timing yourself for a distance that you know is exactly a mile or kilometer, or by walking a quarter of that distance and multiplying your time by four.

On level ground, the average person will walk at a pace of approximately 3 to 4 miles per hour (5 to 6 km/h). Now add in mixed terrain, a backpack, maybe some bad weather, time to look at the map, a few moments here and there to drink water or snack, and that figure will drop a bit more. It'll amount to a rough estimate, but it's still useful—just like it's useful to remember these old calculations from grade school:

D=ST: Distance is equal to speed multiplied by time

T=D/S: Time equals distance divided by speed

S=D/T: Speed is equal to distance multiplied by time

Piloting or Landmarking

Piloting or landmarking is a way of getting around that doesn't require a compass. This is the most common form of navigation and something that you do every day. Piloting is when you navigate by following different features or hopping from a certain landscape to another. You do this when you're making your way around town. For example, "turn right at the end of the street, go over the bridge and past the park and the bank is the tallest building on the street" is a set of directions based on landmarks. Likewise, you can do this by following the features on a map, walking from landmark to landmark and always knowing roughly where you are.

To do this, you need to know where you are on the map to begin with (mark the trailhead on the map before you set out) and where on the map you want to go. Then look for landmarks that you can follow that will keep you on course. These landmarks are called handrails. A handrail can be a river, a long cliff band, the edge of a lake, or even a skidoo trail.

Using a river or shoreline is a great handrail to use as it is easy to spot on a map and as part of the terrain.

WINTER HAZARDS & FIRST AID

In this chapter, I will discuss some potential winter hazards and first aid treatments. However, you must keep in mind that this book is no substitute for professional first aid training. If you are serious about getting into winter backpacking (or wilderness backpacking in general, for that matter), take a wilderness first aid or a wilderness first responder course.

Chapter 7

Dehydration

Hypothermia

Frostbite

Sunburn and Snow Blindness

Immersion Foot

Blisters

Your Winter First Aid Kit

These courses specialize in how to deal with injuries and trauma that can occur in the backcountry and give you hands-on practice in coping with wilderness first aid scenarios. You will learn how to manage everything from sprained ankles and deep cuts to spinal injuries, emergency evacuations and what to do if you or someone in your group falls through ice. These courses are terrific for teaching you how to make do with the supplies you have on hand and the resources you can locate in the field.

It's impossible to be prepared for absolutely every medical situation, but you can try to have what you need to get by in a wide range of common situations. You should start by bringing an ample amount of first aid supplies and having at least a basic knowledge of first aid. The following are some of the basic and most common cold weather injuries and winter hazards—and it's important to note that they can all be completely avoided through proper planning:

- dehydration
- hypothermia
- frostbite
- sunburn
- snow blindness
- immersion foot
- blisters

Dehydration

Dehydration is the loss of fluids (water) from the body. It can happen easily but it's also easy to avoid. Dehydration usually occurs because we do not replenish our body's fluids adequately or quickly enough as we lose water through perspiration, respiration, urination and defecation (sweating, breathing, peeing and bowel movements).

Dehydration results in decreased blood volume. When you have less blood circulating through your body, less heat and fewer nutrients are transported to your organs and extremities, which also makes it harder to digest food that could be used to heat your body. As dehydration advances, your peripheral blood vessels constrict—which limits the flow of warm blood to your fingers, toes and exposed skin—because your body uses its reduced resources to keep your core warm. This process of taking heat from non-vital parts of your body first is called "the shell-to-core shunt." Dehydration can eventually lead to hypothermia.

While side effects will vary depending on the severity of dehydration, they can include weak muscles, low energy, and an altered mental state that typically involves an increasingly negative attitude, decreased motivation and impaired decision-making.

Hypothermia

Hypothermia results when your core temperature drops below its normal temperature. The primary reasons for falling into a hypothermic state are inadequate clothing and protection from the elements, and inadequate food or drink. Illness, fatigue, smoking and the consumption of alcohol can also contribute significantly to the development of hypothermia. Aside from extreme situations, such as getting stuck out in the wilderness unexpectedly or falling into cold water, you should be able to prevent hypothermia by dressing for the weather, planning a proper shelter, drinking and eating regularly, and by watching for and promptly treating the early signs of onset. Hypothermia ranges from mild to severe, with severe hypothermia sometimes causing death.

To avoid or treat dehydration, you need to replace or top up your fluids by drinking regularly throughout your waking hours.

Mild Hypothermia

Your body's normal core temperature is 98.6°F (37°C). As soon as your body's core temperature drops 1.8°F (about 1°C), you enter the first stage of hypothermia. Mild hypothermia is recognizable by some of the following symptoms: chills and shivering, numb skin, loss of dexterity in the hands, and increasing numbness in the extremities as your body performs the shell–core shunt to keep your vital organs as warm as possible.

Mild hypothermia can come with similar side effects to dehydration, namely: feelings of weakness or low energy, tired muscles, negative attitude, impaired judgment and low motivation. If you are treating someone else for mild hypothermia, it can be helpful to remember that their bad mood is probably due to their medical condition!

To quickly recover from mild hypothermia, immediately remove any wet or damp clothes and replace them with dry ones. Then add some more layers of clothing to better protect yourself from wind or precipitation. If you have access to a shelter, remove yourself from the elements completely until you feel better.

The next most important step is to rehydrate with very sweet drinks, which will give your body the energy to generate some heat. Sports drinks are a great option because they help bring body fluids back to normal levels, as well as replacing any electrolytes that have been lost, which will speed recovery and increase your energy. The temperature of the drink does not matter very much, although warmer drinks are more palatable.

Sweet food or simple carbohydrates that can be quickly digested and turned into energy can stoke the internal furnace and help your body to start producing heat, but should be eaten after the consumption of sweet, warm fluids. As you start to feel better, eat something a little more substantial so that you can stabilize your blood sugar.

It used to be recommended that people with mild hypothermia move around to warm up, but exercise has been shown to have a greater "after drop" than fueling the body with sugars. After drop refers to the phenomenon by which the body's core temperature continues to go down for a short period after it has been restored to warmer conditions (for example, bringing a cold person into a warm room and changing their clothes).

Drinking multiple cups of sugared coffee, tea, or hot chocolate will help replace fluids and provide the fuel needed for your body to warm itself.

Moderate and Severe Hypothermia

As hypothermia gets worse, it gets harder to treat. Moderate hypothermia occurs when your body temperature drops below 95°F (about 35°C), and its side effects include a decrease in muscular coordination, confusion, combativeness, and pallor; fingers, toes, ears and lips may become blue. People in this state sometimes become so confused and irrational that they start to remove clothing and even resist treatment. Shivering becomes much more violent. This stage of hypothermia is a serious condition and

Don't cross ice unless you're sure it can hold the weight of you, your group and all your gear. Check with locals and do some research into what the weather in the area has been like for the last few weeks before heading out. It might be cold at the time of your trip, but if it has been warm in the region for the last few weeks, the ice might have become dangerously thin.

ideally would be avoided by recognizing and treating the symptoms of mild hypothermia promptly.

Severe hypothermia begins when your body temperature drops below 89.6°F (about 32°C). In most cases, it overtakes you slowly through gradual and unmitigated heat loss; even if you are immersed in cold water, it can take up to an hour for severe hypothermia to develop.

On the way to severe hypothermia, violent shivering will exhaust the body and stop. Muscles will become stiff and rigid; the patient will be unable to walk, or will walk in an unstable stagger. Skin will become cold and pale, and the patient will progressively suffer from a severely altered mental state, confusion, slurred speech, and might become hostile, irrational and belligerent.

Before transporting a severely hypothermic person, make a human burrito out of any available sleeping bags and tarp or fly and fill it with warm water bottles. This will prevent further heat loss, but immediate medical attention is a must.

When severe hypothermia sets in, the patient will typically fall unconscious or barely respond to voice or pain stimulation, and may stop breathing. For these reasons, treatment must be swift. Do not underestimate this situation: severe hypothermia is a serious emergency requiring immediate evacuation and medical intervention.

Treatment in the field is a stop-gap that must be administered while waiting for professional medical assistance to arrive. Below 86°F (about 30°C), the heart can stop working properly and jostling of the patient can trigger ventricular fibrillation, a medical emergency that can lead to death. Furthermore, the patient cannot be warmed up in the field because their recovery will require professional medical intervention. For these reasons, treatment in the field must involve only the most gentle and careful handling of the patient and be focused on preventing any further heat loss. Start by removing the patient from the elements as soon as possible and remove all wet or damp clothing (using scissors or a knife to cut them off if required to minimize jostling of the patient).

The next step is to make a hypo-wrap, sometimes referred to as a human burrito, to prevent further heat loss. Get the person into a warm sleeping bag and put a hat on them. If you have a tarp or large piece of plastic, place it on the ground, and then put your thickest sleeping pad in the middle on an angle. Think of the plastic as a baseball diamond instead of a square, and orient the sleeping pad in line between second base and home plate. Carefully lift the patient in their sleeping bag and place them on the pad. If you have extra sleeping bags, you can gently wrap these around them. You can also do limited re-warming by filling bottles with hot water, covering them with socks and applying them specifically to the thorax (the upper torso). Finally, wrap the tarp around the person to keep the whole human bundle well-insulated.

Frostbite

Frostbite is the freezing of skin or tissue cells which can lead to tissue death and the possible loss of limbs or digits. Due to the way our bodies react to cold, frostbite typically affects the extremities and areas that are exposed.

The first stages of frostbite are referred to as frost nip. The tell-tale signs of frost nip are very cold fingers, toes, ears or nose, which will start to hurt as the blood flow slows to these areas and the tissues start to freeze. Affected areas may feel swollen or bigger than usual, and will take on a white, waxy look and feel. In most cases of frost nip, the affected areas will be red and swollen for a few days after thawing, but there will be no permanent damage. The swelling is the result of fluid leaking out of the endothelial cells that line blood vessels. Ice crystals form in and between cells, expanding as the area freezes.

By now you have probably noticed that there is often a snowball effect with cold-weather hazards. For example, dehydration can lead to hypothermia and/or frostbite. These afflictions are ugly—avoid them through simple prevention!

Frostbite, more serious than frost nip, can affect larger areas, such as a whole hand or foot, ear, nose or cheek. The severity of frostbite can be partly gauged by how rigid the affected area has become, and whether it is still painful or has reached a point of total numbness. With superficial frostbite, the skin is firm but still has some pliability, and will appear white or gray. Deep frostbite, which has gone beyond the skin to affect muscle, bone, tendon or blood vessels, will still appear white or gray but because deeper structures have been affected; the skin will become hard like wood, with no pliability.

The treatment for frostbite depends on whether it is superficial or deep. Superficial frostbite (frost nip) should have no post-warming complications aside from possible blister formation, though the area may be more susceptible to frostbite in the future. To treat frost nip, skin-to-skin rewarming is best. It's then important to keep the area warm and dry, while minimizing further exposure or refreezing of the area.

To treat deep frostbite properly, you must have ideal conditions for the re-warming. Transport becomes treatment, which means you need to evacuate the person and get them to professional medical attention.

No matter what the condition, NEVER EVER thaw areas that are at risk of being re-frozen or that will be subsequently subjected to pressure, stress, or impact because all these things will result in more extensive, possibly permanent damage to the tissues. For example, it is much better to walk out on a frozen foot than to walk out on a thawed one (which will be excruciating if it is even possible). It is also very important that you never rub frost-nipped or frost-bitten areas, as this may also cause more tissue damage.

The true severity of frostbite is often revealed a few hours, or even days after the area has thawed. A deeply frost-bitten area will develop blisters filled with clear or bloody pus and turn reddish-purple, blue or black. Severely frost-bitten areas often take up to two months to heal. In the worst-case scenario, surgery is required to amputate and remove tissues that are permanently damaged.

Sunburn and Snow Blindness

Just because it is cold or cloudy out doesn't mean that you can't get sunburned. The reflection of sunlight from snow and ice almost doubles the rays you are exposed to, making you that much more susceptible to sunburn. Of course, sunburn is easy to avoid; simply slather exposed skin with a good sunblock that has an SPF rating of 30 or more, and reapply as needed. Wear a hat with a brim to help shade your nose and face from the sun, and always wear sunglasses to protect your eyes from UV rays.

Without sunglasses, a bright day on the snow can have you squinting for hours, followed by a nasty tension headache. Even worse, you can sunburn your eyes, which

On long trips you may want to bring an extra pair in case your sunglasses get damaged or lost; otherwise, if you lose your glasses you can create some Inuit-style snow goggles with anything that will block most of the light to your eyes and give you a narrow slit to peer through.

causes what is known as snow blindness. Snow blindness can be very painful and leave you bedridden and in significant discomfort for days. While I've never experienced it, a friend described it as feeling like someone has taken a handful of beach sand and rubbed it into your eyeballs. It's so easy to avoid this by simply wearing good sunglasses when it is bright out.

Immersion Foot

Immersion foot, also known by some as trench foot, is a condition that arises when feet have been damp for extended periods of time without sufficient exposure to air. Lack of oxygen to the area affects the nerves in your feet and can be very painful. If you suffer immersion foot on a winter camping trip, it is likely to be only a mild case, indicated by tingly, itchy feet that look wrinkled and red or swollen. Immersion foot is not necessarily about being cold, but in the winter, cold feet are often damp feet.

Full recovery from immersion foot is typical, but extreme cases (which are very unlikely on a winter trip because they are caused by days of continuously damp, un-aired feet) can lead to gangrene and require amputation. Immersion foot is very easy to avoid by simply changing into dry socks every evening or any time during the day that your feet have been damp for extended periods. In the warmth and comfort of your shelter in the evening, it's also a good idea to air and dry out your feet a bit before donning new socks. These precautions will also help protect your feet against frostbite, blisters, and general discomfort.

The reflection of the sun off the snow can really take its toll on your eyes, and so a good, dark pair of sunglasses are important to have.

Blisters

We have all had a blister at one time or another in our lives, and know that they can be very distracting, painful and even debilitating. Blisters are often caused by a new or improperly fitting pair of boots, or by socks that rub or chafe. Fortunately, blisters are easy to prevent. If you intend to wear new boots on a winter outing, be sure to break them in by wearing them on a few shorter day hikes first to discover what spots experience friction or discomfort. Try to keep your feet as dry as possible and at the first sign of a hot spot, stop, clean and dry your feet. You should then cover the spot with moleskin or a piece of medical tape before it can turn into a blister. (Like many others, I prefer to simply use duct tape instead of medical tape because it's tough, inexpensive and easy to use. Just be aware that for some people, the adhesive on duct tape can cause a bit of a skin reaction, though it's pretty rare.) After a blister has boiled up, pad it well with gauze and protect it with bandages so that it can reduce on its own. You can also consider a controlled draining of a blister if you think it is likely to be sloughed off anyway. If you drain a blister or one bursts on its own, treat it as you would a cut, applying antibiotic ointment and changing bandages regularly.

Your Winter First Aid Kit

There is no single combination of first aid supplies that is the best, and no kit is a substitute for lack of first aid knowledge. Before putting together your kit, you should at the very least know how to deal with basic first aid scenarios. Remember, by exercising good planning and practicing prevention, you should be able to leave your first aid kit in your bag the entire trip, but always go prepared for the worst!

Use a waterproof and easily identifiable bag for your first aid kit. Red bags designed for this purpose are available at many outdoor shops. Store your first aid kit in a spot that's easy to access, such as in the lid of your backpack or at the top of your pack under the lid.

The following list is a suggestion of what you might want to bring with you for a couple of nights out. Adjust quantities to suit the size of your group. Sometimes it helps to organize things by grouping similar things (like gauze, or bandages) in smaller sealable baggies.

Instead of bringing a bulky roll of duct tape, wrap a long strip around your water bottle. It will be easy to find and take up less space!

Take the time on trail to stop and attend to any hot spots before a full blown blister develops by taping over any area that has extra friction.

- ❏ personal medications or prescriptions (find out before you go which ones do not tolerate freezing, and plan to store these somewhere warmer if required)

- ❏ note pad and pencil (for recording serious incidents and details about the progression of any medical conditions)

- ❏ small lighter

- ❏ pain killers/anti-inflammatory drugs (acetaminophen and ibuprofen, respectively)

- ❏ anti-diarrhea medication

- ❏ package of antihistamines (like Benadryl, in case of allergic reactions)

- ❏ 2 pairs latex gloves

- ❏ sealable plastic bag for hygienic disposal of bandages

- ❏ tube of antibacterial ointment (this may freeze)

- ❏ 1 pair small tweezers

- ❏ 4 antiseptic wipes (benzalkonium chloride)

- ❏ strip of medical tape or duct tape (for blisters)

- ❏ 1 roll of medical tape

- ❏ 3 2x2-inch sterile gauze bandages

- ❏ 3 3x3-inch sterile gauze bandages

- ❏ 3 4x4-inch sterile gauze bandages

- ❏ 1 roll of gauze

- ❏ 1 package skin closures (like Steri-Strip)

- ❏ 4 butterfly closures

- ❏ 3 3x3-inch clear waterproof bandages (like Tegaderm)

- ❏ 1 4x4-inch sterile pressure bandage

- ❏ 1 tampon (these provide excellent absorbency)

- ❏ 1 roll waterproof self-adhesive bandage (like Coban, which can also be used as a tensor for compression)

- ❏ 1 triangular bandage with safety pins

- ❏ assortment of adhesive bandages for minor cuts

WINTER SURVIVAL

When you head out to go winter backpacking, it's wise to keep in mind the old proverb: Hope for the best; prepare for the worst. In fact, winter camping is a lot like a preplanned survival situation. It all comes down the basics: shelter, water, food, and a sense of where you are.

Chapter 8

Leave a Trip Plan

Nine Steps to Survival

Emergency Shelters

Survival Kit

What can turn this controlled and preplanned survival situation into a real survival situation is the element of unpredictability, when you find yourself in a situation that you did not anticipate and for which you are not prepared, and that has potentially serious or fatal consequences.

The most common problems that can develop into survival situations are: getting lost or disoriented, equipment failure, unexpected bad weather or a disabling injury. Basically, survival comes into play in any situation where you cannot make it back to civilization before your resources run out or become inadequate.

A classic example is when someone heads out snowshoeing for a couple of hours with only what they are wearing and enough water and snacks for the afternoon, but then gets lost and has to spend an unexpected night out. In truly epic survival situations, the outcome often comes down to the will to live, and maybe a bit of luck.

The good news is, you can easily improve your odds of survival with a little preparation and know-how.

Leave a Trip Plan

Before you go into the bush, no matter how short the trip, always tell a reliable friend or family member exactly where you are planning to go and when you intend to be back.

For longer trips, take your detailed trip planning notes, organize them and type them up, and attach your meal and equipment packing lists so potential rescuers will have information about everything you have with you. A thorough trip plan for an overnight trip should cover as many what-ifs as possible and provide some helpful information such as:

If there's nobody around when you head out, even if it's just for a winter walk in the woods, leave a note behind in an obvious place for someone to find. That way if you get into trouble and are overdue, someone will know that you're missing and where to look for you.

- Who to call and what to do if you're not back by a certain time.
- The number of people in your party, their names and any medical conditions.
- Useful names and numbers, like local search and rescue, and next of kin.
- Your planned route and any alternate routes you might take.
- Coordinates of your proposed campsites.
- What you have with you, including any communication or signaling devices like a cell phone or a whistle.
- Identifying information such as the colors of your tents.

This is the cheapest form of travel insurance and will give you some peace of mind knowing that help will be on the way if you can't make it home. Of course, it's equally important to let people know when you return, so nobody calls in search and rescue when you're already back on a friend's couch with a bowl of popcorn.

Nine Steps to Survival

When things do go wrong, there are some basic steps to remember that will help you analyze the situation and take the appropriate action.

1. Accept the Situation

Accept the fact that you are lost or in trouble and will need find a solution or stay out longer than you planned. If you are lost, don't fight the situation by wandering in circles trying to find your way out; you will probably only get more lost and make it harder for someone to find you. Instead, stay in one spot. If someone is injured, your panicking will not help. Try to stay calm and focused. You'll be able to think more clearly and come up with a plan to stay alive and survive.

2. Conserve Your Energy

You need energy to survive and keep warm, and depending on the situation, you may not have much food with you, so try not to waste energy by running around. The basic necessities in life are shelter, water and food, in that order, and you need to direct all your energy toward these things first.

3. Take Inventory

Go through everything you have with you and on you. How much food and water do you have? How long will it last? How much clothing do you have to keep you warm? What can you use to make a fire; a shelter?

Being mentally prepared for a survival situation often makes the difference between surviving and making poor choices that stem from anxiety. It's important to try and remain calm from the first moment that you realize you're in trouble.

One way to melt snow is to sprinkle it out on black or dark-colored plastic bag, or even a black snowshoe, and leave it out in the sun. Dark colors absorb more heat from the sun's rays and although it can be slow, it will work to melt snow in small quantities, which is better than nothing! You can also put a little snow inside your dark plastic bag and leave it out in the sun. The interior of the bag will heat up like a little greenhouse and melt the snow.

4. Find or Make a Shelter

Making or finding a shelter is your first priority. You may not get much sleep, if any, but you will need something to protect you from the elements, to help you conserve as much heat as possible. You should be able to make a sufficient shelter for an evening in one to one-and-a-half hours. Your shelter doesn't have to be a work of art; it just needs to function (remember the mechanisms of heat loss). While building your shelter, adjust your layers to make sure you don't build up a sweat and get damp, which will only speed up your heat loss.

In a survival situation, it's worth it to take a bit more time to prepare your fire ingredients so that it will light and catch more quickly, allowing you to conserve your matches and fuel.

If you don't have a lighter or other conventional means of lighting a fire, you can use prescription eye glasses, a magnifying glass, binoculars or even a camera lens to concentrate the sun's rays and start a fire.

5. Get Water

Once you have constructed a suitable shelter, you should have a more relaxed state of mind knowing that you have somewhere to retreat to. Next, look for a water source. Otherwise, you may have to resort to using snow. Keep any liquid water you have from freezing so you don't have to use energy to thaw it later; keep your water bottle inside your jacket. Conserve your water but make sure you are still drinking regularly if you can. It is surprisingly common for people who have gotten lost to be found severely dehydrated but with a full bottle of water.

6. Get Food

Food is your next priority. Take an inventory of your food and think about how you will ration it. Foraging for food in the winter can be very difficult, so hopefully you have at least a small portion of food that you can ration to get you by until you are rescued. One important thing to note about food: staying hydrated is more important than staying fed—you can survive for days or weeks without food—so if you have minimal water, try not to eat too much. Your body uses water to digest, so if you're low on water, eating will dehydrate you faster. Eat in relation to how much water you have.

7. Light a Fire

Fire is extremely useful in survival situations. The heat from a fire will provide a great deal of comfort and reduce the amount of energy you spend to stay warm. It will keep your hands and feet warm and, built properly, heat the inside of your shelter. You can also use a fire as a signaling device for a rescue. A fire can be a great psychological comfort, fighting loneliness and stoking your will to survive. Finally, fire is the ingredient you need to melt snow for drinking water—and you can survive a long time without food as long as you can stay warm and keep drinking. In a survival situation you can bend the no-trace rules and snap dead branches off trees, peel off birch bark—whatever it takes to get a blaze going.

8. Stay Covered

Wear as many layers as needed or as possible, remembering to keep your head and neck covered to prevent the substantial heat loss from these areas. Also take care of your hands and feet; keep the blood flowing to prevent frostbite. Keeping your hands and feet warm will in turn help keep your core warmer.

9. Signal for Help

Create some form of a signal. A big, bright fire at night is a great way to been seen. If someone is searching for you and they know your general whereabouts, this can be enough to pinpoint your location. During the day, throw green or rotting wood on your fire to send up smoke that can be seen from miles away. Just be careful not to smother it in the process!

No matter how thirsty you are, do not be tempted to eat snow. The energy cost of melting snow with your body heat is far greater than the benefit of the tiny amount of water you'll get out of it. Think about how much energy it takes for your stove to melt a full pot of snow–A LOT–and how much you end up with at the bottom of the pot –barely any!

The number three in any form is a distress signal, so spacing three fires out in a large triangle shape is one way to make sure that people know you're in trouble. If you have a whistle, three short loud consecutive blasts is the audio signal for distress. A loud whistle, the kind without a little ball in it, can be heard for a long distance. Repeat whistle blasts frequently and listen carefully for a response. If you do hear something, keep blowing your whistle until rescuers find you.

If you have a mirror or something else reflective you can try using it to signal passing aircraft with reflected sunlight.

Emergency Shelters

You already have most of the information you need to build an emergency shelter. Most of the possible designs—lean-tos, coffin shelters, trench shelters, quinzees and snow caves—have been covered in detail in Chapter 5. Your goal is to build the warmest shelter you can while expending the least energy possible, keeping in mind the principles of heat conservation. In Chapter 1 we discussed the mechanisms of heat loss: conduction, convection, radiation and evaporation. When constructing a shelter, no matter what type, keep these mechanisms in mind and take precautions against each one of them. Here are some examples of ways you can do this.

• *To minimize heat loss through conduction*, keep yourself off the ground. If you don't have a sleeping pad with you, find something else to get your body off the ground, like evergreen boughs, your backpack or other gear—anything you can find that doesn't conduct heat very well. If you have sticks and logs, you can build a platform, using boughs for padding.

• *To minimize heat loss through convection*, cut down on drafts by plugging all of the holes of your shelter with snow. Remember that you only need a few holes the size of a golf ball for ventilation.

• *To minimize heat loss through radiation*, build your walls as solidly as possible, with little extra space around your body, so that they can reflect back the heat that comes off your body.

• *To minimize heat loss through evaporation*, stay calm and be careful not to work up a sweat building your shelter.

Backpack Bivy

There are some tricks you can use to augment your shelter or stay a little bit warmer if you aren't able to build one. One of these is the backpack bivy.

If you have a backpack with a floating or a removable lid and an extendable snow collar, you can slide up three quarters of your body into the pack, depending on its size. You

A good method for creating an emergency mattress is to cut as many evergreen boughs as you can and then cover them with your backpack.

can also use this method inside of any emergency shelter that you construct, to help you to retain some body heat, protect a portion of your body from the elements as well as create a bit of a barrier between you and the ground. If you can't build any kind of shelter, well, this is better than nothing.

The Body Huddle

If all other resources fail and you are unable to construct an adequate shelter for the evening—or even if you can but are still cold—you can resort to basically hugging yourself. Put on as many layers as you have (make sure that all the layers together are not too restricting as this will only make you colder) and cover your head and neck. Sit on something to protect you from losing heat to the ground through conduction. Tuck your knees tight to your chest, hug your arms around your knees, and put your face into your lap. If your jacket or parka is big enough, you can try pulling it over your knees and pulling your sleeves and arms inside as well. Be sure to pull the drawstrings tight around the bottom of your jacket to reduce heat loss. If you're in a group, you can all huddle together like this.

Survival Kit

You can never carry enough for every possible situation, but you can put together a small survival kit that is easy to toss into your pack anytime you're heading out, be it for an hour or a week. With these essentials, plus some knowledge and creativity, your chances of survival will increase greatly.

Along with its traditional use, you can strap your headlamp to a water bottle to create a handy little freestanding lantern.

Survival Kit

- ❏ *fire (waterproof matches, lighter or other fire starter)*
- ❏ *bright orange plastic garbage bag for signaling; black garbage bag for melting snow; both can also be helpful for making shelters*
- ❏ *very loud whistle (preferably one without a little ball in it, which can rust)*
- ❏ *15 feet (5m) of parachute cord or 3mm accessory cord*
- ❏ *multi-tool or sharp knife*
- ❏ *extra fleece or wool hat*
- ❏ *candle*
- ❏ *compass (always take a bearing before you wander off)*
- ❏ *small LED flashlight with fresh batteries*
- ❏ *first aid kit*
- ❏ *energy food*
- ❏ *small mirror*
- ❏ *plastic zip ties*

Good Company: Kids & Dogs

Chapter 9

Winter Backpacking with Children

Winter Backpacking with Dogs

It might seem funny to lump kids and dogs together in one chapter, but I figured that since they are both special kinds of company that can enhance a winter backpacking trip and require particular consideration, why not?

Winter Backpacking with Children

Backpacking and camping can be two of the most enjoyable activities for parents and kids to share together. It's an opportunity for quality bonding time that will result in many great memories.

For the most part, all the information in this book applies to children as much as adults. There are just a few extra considerations and precautions to take into account when you're winter backpacking with kids.

Know Their Limits

You should try winter camping on your own one or two times before you bring kids along. Winter camping is already challenging by itself. Bringing your kids along on your first outing might be too much of a challenge, resulting in a bad experience and souring your outlook on the whole activity.

After you're got your systems worked out from a bit of experience and you have a good handle on the art of winter camping, you can then consider inviting the kids. Just be realistic about what you and your kids can handle together. Teenagers can handle most of the same challenges as adults. But if a child won't be able to walk the whole distance on their own, or is not old enough to walk, it's probably not a good idea to take them winter camping, especially on a trip where the weather can drop below freezing during the day.

Extremities—hands, feet, head—are top priorities when dressing children for winter camping so it's a good idea to opt for mitts with dummy strings.

Kids love the snow, and they also have a seemingly endless reserve of energy—great qualities for the world of winter camping.

Kids' Clothing

Just like teens and adults, children should also be dressing in layers as outlined in Chapter 1. You may want your child dressed a little on the cool side when first heading out. They'll soon be running around in the snow and you don't want to be too conservative and bundle them up so much that they'll be sweating and soaking all their warm clothes. If they haven't warmed up after 15 minutes, add an extra layer or two.

Boots and Socks

Make sure that your child has a fully insulated and preferably waterproof winter boot that is about one size too big. This should allow enough room inside to wiggle their toes with socks on and boots tied up. The worst thing that can happen is too much restriction that will impede blood flow, leading to cold feet, frost nip and ultimately frostbite. For the same reason it's also important not to put on more than one pair of socks or socks that are too thick. The best sock is a medium-thick wool or synthetic sock. Stay away from the cotton socks they got from Grandma at Christmas—never wear cotton socks!

Frostbite Check

Every half hour or so, do a fingers, nose, ears and toes check. Ask your child if their fingers and toes are warm and if they can feel them. Ask them to wiggle their fingers and toes. Slip off their mittens and do a visual check for frost nip or frostbite (see Chapter 8 for the signs and symptoms) on hands, then check ears and nose. I don't recommend taking off boots unless they say their toes really hurt or they can't feel them; it's best to minimize any exposure to the cold air and wind.

Food and Water

Keeping your child topped up with food and water will give them all the energy they need to make it through a cold and adventurous day and night. Adequate hydration and nutrition will help keep them as warm as possible, keep their bodies and muscles working proficiently, keep their spirit and attitude more positive and reduce the chances of frostbite. Follow the advice in Chapter 2 for winter nutrition and hydration.

Monitor their fluid intake and encourage them to drink as much as possible. Try to make a game out of it and offer a prize: Who can drink two bottles of water by dinner tonight? You can even have a peeing contest. Who can pee the most during the day? Checking the color of their urine is a great way to see if they are staying hydrated. The general rule is that urine should be clear and copious.

What Kids Can Carry

Don't overload your child with more gear than is appropriate for their age and size. Winter camping will already be a challenge. If they are able to carry their water, some

Pack lots of tasty snacks and treats that you know the kids like so they'll have every reason to eat throughout the day.

snacks and their sleeping bag, that's great. Having them carry the bulkier but lighter-weight sleeping bag will leave you room to carry the extra food and other gear they won't be carrying.

Kids' Backpacks

Any pack that is big enough to hold a sleeping bag and snacks and has padded and comfortable shoulder straps will work fine. It should not be too big and cumbersome for their body. Since they won't be carrying a lot of weight, a big load-bearing hip belt is not mandatory, but a waist stabilizer will be an asset to keep the pack from sliding around. If the pack doesn't have either, you can always sew a couple of pieces of extra webbing onto the pack and add a plastic clip. It only needs to be strong enough to keep the pack from sliding side to side.

Keeping kids warm at night is easily achieved by using a sleeping system that is rated for the conditions, appropriate clothing, and tucking an insulated hot water bottle into the bag.

Fill a child's bag with lightweight items like a sleeping bag and some snacks. These things aren't too heavy and will give them a feeling of responsibility and accomplishment.

Pint-Sized Sleeping Systems

You may need to search around a bit to find a sleeping bag small enough for your child especially one with a good enough temperature rating. The right size leaves no more than a foot of extra room at the end of the sleeping bag because you don't want to have too much dead air space that their body will have to heat up. If the bag does have more than a foot at the bottom, fill it at night with their clothing, even their dry clothes, which will ensure everything is warm for the morning. As for sleeping pads, you can get them in kids' sizes if you like, or just use an adult-sized one. If you use a plain foam one, you can cut it down to their body length to save weight and bulk.

In your shelter, let kids sleep between adults so that you can share your body heat with them and keep them away from the colder outside edges. If your child's sleeping bag is the same size as yours, you can sometimes zip the two sleeping bags together, add an extra fleece blanket to fill in some of the draft holes, and then snuggle together for the night.

While you might consider it optional for yourself, always put a water bottle filled with hot water and then wrapped in a thick sock in a kid's sleeping bag before bed. A cozy hat with a drawstring (to help keep it on their head) is also a must.

Winter Backpacking with Dogs

It's not always easy to just drop everything and take off backpacking. You've got time off work, but who's going to take care of the dog? Fortunately, dogs were made to live in the outdoors. They love to go outside and play in the snow. They love going for walks. They probably love sleeping in your bed when you let them. So why not have more excitement and company on your winter adventure and bring your canine friend(s) to share in the experience?

Food and Water

Dogs are animals just like you are, of course. So, just like you, they'll need to eat more in the winter because they'll be burning extra energy to stay warm and move through the snow, and they'll need to drink more because they'll be losing moisture to the dry air.

You've probably got your dog's regular diet already figured out. For a winter trip, increase this regular amount by 25%, and also pack some extra treats for rewards and snacks between meals. Make sure your dog is drinking frequently and abundantly. Every time that you stop for a drink break, make sure that your dog gets a drink too. Keep a travel dish that is made of either a durable pet-safe plastic or a collapsible one made of material at the top of your pack (or your dog's) to make this easy and convenient. Likewise, they will need food to burn as fuel and energy, and having a good stash of snacks that you can bust out every now and then will help to keep your furry friend warmer and topped up with energy.

There are plenty of collapsible dog bowls on the market that make camping with your dog a breeze and are also good to just have stowed in your car for drink breaks on the road.

Dog Packs

Since your dog will need an ample supply of food and water, and maybe a bit of extra gear, you might want to consider having him carry his fair share of the load. Dogs can carry about a quarter of their bodyweight in a properly fitted pair of saddle bags—that's a lot less weight on your legs! These are just like the saddle bags for a bike, motorcycle or horse. They come in pairs with one bag for each side.

The best packs for your dog will take into account proper padding in high rub areas (under buckles, under belly) and breathability.

When choosing saddle bags for your pup, shop around and bring your dog to try them on. Find ones that fit properly. If you have the opportunity and your dog will let you (this being the first time it has had the pack on), fill up the bags, keeping the weight even. Get your pooch to walk around with the pack on, sit and lie down. Check that there's lots of clearance between the bags and the ground, that there's no rubbing or restriction behind the legs and around the belly, and that your dog will still be able to go to the bathroom.

Do some pre-trip training before you take your dog out overnight. Fit the dog with the empty saddle bags before going out to walk or play. Your dog will get used to wearing something on his back and he'll start associating the bags with a fun activity. Slowly start to add weight until you're ready for the big overnighter.

When you load saddle bags, make sure that you pack the same weight and volume in each one. Also make sure that there are no hard or sharp lumps poking through the backside into your dog's belly or ribs. After every training walk, check your dog for hot spots where the bag might be rubbing excessively and make any necessary adjustments before irritations and blisters can occur. It's also a good idea to check with your vet about your dog's health before loading him up.

In my opinion, it's not fair to load up a dog with anything more than its own food, water and gear. But as long as you're not overloading your pooch, what you give them is up to you. Whatever you decide, be aware that a dog will be a lot less careful with its load than you'll be with yours. Gear that you don't want to get damaged when your dog goes crashing through the forest after rabbits should stay with you; and anything in the dog's pack that you want to stay dry should be double-bagged and well sealed.

Dogs don't need a lot of extra gear, and you should be able to fit most or all of what they'll need into their saddle bags. Here's a sample packing list for your dog:
• dog food
• dog water rations (in an insulated bottle so it doesn't freeze)
• drinking bowl
• dog collar and leash or extra rope
• closed-cell foam pad for sleeping and rest stops
• blanket for nighttime
• favorite toy
• extra treats and snacks
• fleece neck guard for cold days
• glow stick or headlamp for dog collar at night
• paw salve or booties if needed

To make a great winter snack for your dog, buy the soft dog food that comes in rolls (like Rollover or Natural Balance), and then chop some up and pack it into a bag before the trip. Mix the meaty morsels with hot water to make a belly-warming stew—which they'll appreciate right before bed.

Winterizing Your Dog's Paws

One of the first things people usually worry about is if their pooch's feet are going to freeze solid during the day and how they will fare out overnight. Dogs are well adapted to deal with fluctuations in weather and temperature; that's one reason why they often shed in the spring and summer and grow a thicker coat in the winter. But there are still things to be aware of and prepare for.

This has probably happened to you before. You're out on a walk, notice that your dog is favoring a paw, trying to keep it off the ground, and you think it's too cold out. But it's more likely that ice balls have built up in the dog's paws, holding cold and moisture against the skin. Most dogs have long fur between their toes that can cover the pads of their paws for protection and warmth, and body heat can melt this snow and cause ice balls to build up in the fur. This is one reason your dog may be chewing and licking away at its paws after a winter walk.

Also, if you live in a place where the roads are heavily salted and slushy, salt can irritate your dog's paws and cause them to dry out and crack. Your dog will like to lick the salt off, which isn't the healthiest of treats.

There are a few things that you can do to avoid these problems:

1. Trim the hair between your dog's toes short to prevent snow and ice from balling up. This will help prevent frostbite and prevent slipping on ice.

2. Cut nails short and keep them trimmed to prevent toes from spreading too far apart and trapping snow. This will also keep extra stress and pressure off of paws on harder surfaces.

3. Wash paws thoroughly with warm, fresh water after a walk on salty streets in town. This will remove all the unhealthy salt that your dog will love to lick off and prevent drying and cracking of the pads.

4. If you've been walking in heavily salted and slushy areas, typically urban areas, cover your dog's feet with a specialty dog paw salve, Vaseline or even a coating of cooking spray. This will create a barrier of warmth and moisturize the pads, as well as preventing the snowballing effect. Wipe it off before heading back inside.

5. As an alternative to 3 and 4, above, you can also consider a set of those booties that attach on with Velcro. Booties keep paws warm and dry as well as keeping all of the salt out. It might take a few tries before your dog gets used to them, and hopefully he won't destroy them by trying to chew them off.

Keeping Your Pooch Warm and Happy

In winter temperatures, which can drop below -20°F (-30°C) plus wind-chill, dogs often need more than just their winter fur to keep them warm.

If snowballs appear on your pup's paws, it's time to trim the foot fur.

Like humans, dogs lose a lot of their heat through their neck and head where there's a lot of blood flow. It wouldn't be practical to put a wool hat on your dog but one thing that works well is a fleece neck gaiter. A neck gaiter is comfortable and adds a lot of warmth for minimal weight.

If you have a smaller dog with a coat that is not very thick, consider a fleece or neoprene jacket to cover up his abdomen and chest. You can buy vests, jackets and even full snow

It will be an entertaining show the first time you put booties on your dog. They will prance around taking big, high steps and looking like a four-legged spider

suits with hoods made specifically for dogs. Or, if you are good with a needle and thread, tailor up a sweet new winter jacket or vest of your own.

A buddy of mine puts his dog's lifejacket on him on really cold winter days for extra protection from wind and cold. The lifejacket works great and doubles as a sleeping pad for the dog at night.

Sleeping Warm and Comfortable

Your dog's metabolism will slow down at night, and even though he might have a nice thick coat of fur, there are a few things you can do to ensure his comfort and increase his overall warmth. If you think about it, these are exactly the same things you need to do for yourself:

1. Make sure your dog pees before bed so his body doesn't waste energy keeping his pee warm all night. This will also ensure that you both have a better night's sleep because you won't have to wake up to let him out.

2. Give him a snack before bed so he has energy to keep warm.

3. Bring a closed-cell pad to protect him from the cold ground. You can also use your empty pack as an extra layer of protection.

There are entire doggy sleeping systems available in pet stores and online—everything from camp cots to sleeping bags. Just be sure to assess your real needs and carrying capacity before investing.

A neck gaiter or lifejacket can really help keep your dog warm on cold days.

4. Put his neck warmer on.

5. Give him a light fleece blanket for additional warmth. Or, if you are camping with someone else and you have room in your shelter, have your dog sleep between you. The dog won't need a blanket because the overlap from the two sleeping bags will be enough. And you'll both benefit from some nice radiating dog heat!

Doggie Etiquette

Before your trip, make sure that dogs are allowed where you're going. Be prepared to pick up after him if need be. If there are going to be other campers around, be sure that your dog will listen to your commands and won't bother them by barking. If heading out on a trail, keep the dog from interfering with other travelers and from disturbing groomed ski tracks by walking in them. Carry a leash or a length of rope to tie the dog up in case you have to. Finally, make sure that your dog has tags on his collar with his name, your address and your phone number in case you get separated out there.

You may know your dog will not bite or bother anyone else but on high traffic trails it is simply respectful of others to keep your dog on a leash.

PLAN YOUR TRIP AND DO IT!

Every great thing in life begins with an idea, a vision or a dream. Successful people are the ones who act on their dreams and ideas; they don't just sit around and talk about them. Trip planning works the same way.

Get Out There and Camp!

The first step is easy—it's your spark of excitement, your dream of adventure. But the next step doesn't have to be hard either. If you use the information in this book, you will have the knowledge you need to follow through and make your winter backpacking dream happen. Now you just have to bring it all together, get out there and do it!

I like to start off by settling down in someplace comfy with a strong, tasty cup of my favorite dark roast, a few sheets of paper and a pen, and pondering some questions. These are some of the important things you need to ask yourself to advance from dream to reality:

• What are my goals and objectives of the trip? (For example: To spend one full night out in the bush? To explore a certain area? Or simply to stay dry and warm, have a good time, and not go hungry?)

• Are these goals in line with my skills and experience?

• How long do I want to stay out? How much time do I have?

- When do I want to go?

- Where do I want to go? Is that area a good place for what I want to do?

- How will I get there?

- What will the weather be like in that area at that time? How cold might it get? What has the weather been like in the area for the last few weeks?

- What type of terrain will I be camping in?

Always choose your travel companions wisely and be honest with each other about skill levels and goals while trip planning.

- Am I in good enough physical condition for this trip?

- Do I need any maps or guidebooks?

- Do I need to make reservations or pay for any permits where I'm going?

- What is my emergency evacuation plan (if something should go wrong or I just want to bail and go home)?

- Do I have a Plan B? Do I need to plan some alternate destinations or routes in case Plan A doesn't work?

- Who will I go with? Will I go solo? Is this a safe option?

- Will I bring the dog or the kids?

- How much food do I need?

- What will I eat?

- What am I going to pack for clothes and equipment?

- Do I need to buy, borrow or rent any clothes or gear?

- How will I stay warm?

- How will I get drinking water?

As you can see, there's a lot to think about, so the sooner you start planning, the better. Obviously the farther away you will be going, the longer you go for and the more people you go with, the more time you'll need at this stage. Allow time to research your route, organize your equipment, buy or rent gear, plan your menu and pack your food. Don't try to do this all at once; break it down into steps. And if you're going with a group, get together and divide up the tasks.

Having extra time to plan and prepare will ensure that you don't feel rushed and will leave you stress free and excited to head out on your adventure. But whatever you do, don't spend a hundred years sitting around planning and thinking. Get out there and camp!

APPENDIX: PACKING LISTS

You can photocopy the following lists, modify them to suit your requirements, and check things off as you lay them out, organize them, and pack them.

* Indicates optional and/or group gear.

Day Hike Gear

- ❏ 25- to 30- liter backpack
- ❏ 2 quarts (2 liters) of water
- ❏ 2000 calories worth of snacks (mostly simple and complex carbs)
- ❏ appropriate active clothing layers (base layer, middle layer, outer layer)
- ❏ insulated or leather hiking boots, or ski boots
- ❏ medium-weight synthetic or wool socks
- ❏ gaiters
- ❏ toque
- ❏ gloves
- ❏ small first aid kit
- ❏ knife or multi-tool

Appendix

Day Hike Gear

Sleeping Gear

Active Clothing

Dry Clothing

Cooking Equipment

Shelter Equipment

Winter-Specific Equipment

Miscellaneous Gear

Personal and Hygiene

- ❏ whistle (Fox 40)
- ❏ sunglasses*
- ❏ topographical map of area and compass

The following items should be brought on day hikes to accommodate the eventuality of having to spend an unexpected night out in the wilderness.

- ❏ L.E.D headlamp
- ❏ small emergency kit (packed in a durable Ziploc bag) that includes a lighter and matches, 15 feet (5m) of 3mm cord, zip ties, duct tape, tea candles, large garbage bag)
- ❏ small, light tarp
- ❏ down or synthetic jacket or parka
- ❏ 1500 calories of emergency snacks
- ❏ 2 x 2 foot piece of closed cell foam (to sit or stand on)
- ❏ extra mitts (warmer than gloves)
- ❏ extra warm toque
- ❏ balaclava

Sleeping Gear

Be sure to bring everything you need for a comfortable sleep, within reason–duvets don't pack or travel well no matter what form of transportation you choose.

- ❏ sleeping bag rated for 5°F (-15°C) or colder
- ❏ stuff sack and waterproofing system
- ❏ closed-cell foam pad
- ❏ inflatable sleeping pad (e.g. Therm-a-Rest or other)*
- ❏ vapor barrier liner (for trips two days or longer)*
- ❏ synthetic over-bag*
- ❏ warm hat that covers ears, preferably with draw cord

Active Clothing

These are the items you'll wear when you head out and during the day every day of your trip, adjusting the layers to keep warm but not sweaty.

- ❏ insulated winter boots (removable liner is an asset)
- ❏ leather hiking boots or plastic mountaineering boots are other possibilities*
- ❏ synthetic T-shirt
- ❏ medium-weight long johns (to wear next to skin)
- ❏ medium-weight long-sleeved top (to wear next to skin)

- ❏ medium-weight insulating layer top
- ❏ medium-weight insulating layer bottom
- ❏ vest
- ❏ shell jacket
- ❏ synthetic or down jacket/parka
- ❏ shell pants
- ❏ synthetic or wool socks
- ❏ vapor barrier socks (grocery bags work too)*
- ❏ warm gloves or mitts
- ❏ warm hat
- ❏ gaiters (if not wearing high-top winter boots)*
- ❏ Any other clothing appropriate for the climate you will be traveling in that you think you will use, but don't overpack!*

Dry Clothing

The clothes you will keep waterproofed no matter what the forecast and change into once you've set up camp for the day.

- ❏ medium or expedition-weight long johns
- ❏ medium or expedition-weight long-sleeved top
- ❏ dry mitts
- ❏ warm hat (your active one will get sweaty)
- ❏ synthetic or down booties*
- ❏ 2 extra pairs wool or synthetic socks
- ❏ neck gaiter or balaclava

Cooking Equipment

Try to nest all of this gear (except for your fuel and water bottles) inside one of your pots and store it all inside its own stuff sack.

- ❏ white gas liquid fuel stove (or whatever stove you have)
- ❏ fuel pump
- ❏ fuel bottle
- ❏ extra fuel and bottle
- ❏ funnel*
- ❏ wind screen
- ❏ bottom heat deflector

- ❏ stove base*
- ❏ pot gripper (you can use your multi-tool instead if you have one)*
- ❏ dish cloth (for wiping out your pot)
- ❏ stove maintenance repair kit (specific to your stove)
- ❏ lighters (pack several)
- ❏ 1-quart (1L) pot with lid
- ❏ multi-tool with pliers (for example, Leatherman)
- ❏ plastic spork
- ❏ insulated plastic mug (used also as a bowl)
- ❏ 2 water bottles, 1-quart (1L) capacity—non-metal and leak-proof
- ❏ water bottle insulators
- ❏ thermos*

Shelter Equipment

- ❏ tent and fly
- ❏ ground sheet/tarp
- ❏ tent pegs (can use sticks or other equipment as a dead man's)*
- ❏ bivy sack*
- ❏ 15 feet (5 meters) of 3-millimeter cord or equivalent*
- ❏ snow shovel
- ❏ tent pole repair sleeve
- ❏ spare zipper slider
- ❏ needle and thread
- ❏ duct tape

Winter-Specific Equipment

- ❏ 4600 cubic inch (75 L) or larger internal frame backpack with load bearing waistbelt*
- ❏ snowshoes*
- ❏ skis*
- ❏ wax kit*
- ❏ ski boots*
- ❏ climbing skins*
- ❏ adjustable ski / trekking poles*
- ❏ avalanche transceiver (required for mountain travel)*
- ❏ probe (required for mountain travel)*

❏ safety shovel (required for mountain travel)*

Miscellaneous Gear

❏ sunglasses (and an extra pair if the trip is on the longer side)

❏ whistle

❏ map

❏ trip plan and emergency action plan

❏ compass

❏ GPS*

❏ short foam pad

❏ headlamp

❏ extra batteries for headlamp and other

❏ repair kit: zip ties, wire, needle and thread, duct tape, spare buckle and webbing, seam sealer, matches, paper clips, 15 feet (5 meters) of 3-millimeter cord, knife, and other odds and sods that you know you might need.

❏ note-book or journal and pencil (ink in pens can freeze)*

❏ book to read*

❏ folding saw*

❏ extra garbage bags and grocery bags and sealable bags (like Ziploc)

❏ watch

❏ camera*

Personal and Hygiene:

❏ first aid kit

❏ sun-screen

❏ toothbrush

❏ toothpaste

❏ bandana

❏ handkerchief

❏ hand sanitizer

❏ toilet paper (pack in a Ziploc with a paper bag and a lighter, remove inner cardboard tube)*

❏ lip balm

THE **HELICONIA PRESS**

For more great books and DVDs on a variety of outdoor activities,
visit *The Heliconia Press* online.
www.helipress.com